Pass It On

THE ASTONISHING STORY OF SAVERS AND VALUE VILLAGE

PAUL GRESCOE

Published by
Tribute Books Inc.
Vancouver, British Columbia
and Toronto, Ontario
www.tributebooks.ca

Library and Archives Canada Cataloguing in Publication

Grescoe, Paul, 1939-
    Pass it on: the astonishing story of Savers and Value Village / Paul Grescoe.

ISBN 0-9732584-4-6

    1. Savers, Inc. – History. 2. Thrift shops – Canada. 3. Thrift shops – United States. 4. Chain stores – Canada. 5. Chain stores – United States. I. Title.

HF5482.4.G63 2005   381'.19   C2005-904382-2

Editor: Audrey Grescoe
Art director: Li-Eng Lodge, Electra Design
Layout and production coordinator: Diane Yee
Cover photography: Getty Images
Printed and bound in Canada by Friesens

Photo credits:
Unless otherwise indicated, photographs in this book are courtesy of Savers Inc. and the families of William Ellison, Herbert Ellison, and Tom Ellison. P. 21, Simon Fraser University; P. 29, Community Services for the Blind and Partially Sighted, Seattle; P. 52 and 56, The Salvation Army National Archives; P. 88, Deni Eagland, *The Vancouver Sun*; P. 128, John Gordon, *Langley Times*; P. 137, Alberta Association for Community Living; P. 196, Canadian Diabetes Association; P. 200, Big Brothers Big Sisters, Long Island, N.Y.

"Village Idiot" lyrics on Page 19 are published with the permission of Jo Miller.

Table of Contents

Acknowledgments

Researching and writing a corporate history that is also a family saga can be a tricky venture. My thanks go first to Tom Ellison, who encouraged the project and gave me unfettered access to Savers Inc. – all its managers and employees – and suggested interviews with those who had left (no matter their reason for leaving) and with critics as well as friends of the company. I'm grateful to founder Bill Ellison for all his memories of the early days and to his brother, Herb, a professional historian who has such vivid recall of the family stories.

All of the men and women at Savers who were interviewed for this book – in the Back Rooms, on the sales floors, and at the corporate office – were patient and helpful. The people representing the charitable organizations involved with the company were also welcoming. There are too many to single out here, but many of their names appear on the following pages.

Several individuals deserve special mention. Brenda Seraphim was my first contact with the company (through the good offices of a mutual friend, Bob McMillin of PriceWaterhouseCoopers in Vancouver) and she offered an enthusiastic and wonderfully well-versed introduction to the characters I'd meet. The knowledgeable Becky Henchman was a vital and gracious liaison with Savers in the initial stages of research until she went on maternity leave. The insightful Ellen Spiess took over from Becky and not only answered my endless questions quickly and thoroughly but also offered thoughtful opinions. Lea Anne Ottinger, as an outside director, proved an articulate commentator on the company and its alliance with Berkshire Partners. Eric Farley and Gina Cohen were invaluable in providing background and laboriously digging through the corporate archives to locate loads of photographs.

The highly creative Li Eng-Lodge of Electra Design of Vancouver was, as usual, a delight to work with in the production and design of the book – as was her talented and diligent colleague, Diane Yee. Ernst Vegt of Coast Imaging Arts of Vancouver rescued some doubtful archival images for us. Jorge Rocha of Friesens of Altona, Manitoba, proved again how good a printer's rep he is. Two fellow islanders were of great assistance: Kim Sinclair displayed her customary skill in transcribing endless hours of tapes, and Lorraine Ashdown interviewed some non-profits' officials and clients for the human stories behind these organizations.

Finally, I'm grateful (indebted, actually) to my wife, the writer and editor Audrey Grescoe, who did detailed on-site research in Savers' stores, combed through decades of archival material, and then edited and proofread the manuscript with her usual polish and intelligence.

Paul Grescoe
Bowen Island, B.C.
August 2005

THE PEOPLE'S STORE

INTRODUCTION

It's the world's most celebrated chain of thrift department stores – a gargantuan garage sale that's run for profit with sophisticated retailing savvy yet returns more than $130 million a year to registered charitable organizations in three countries on two continents.

Forbes, the business magazine, reports the company's stores in the United States "look more like Wal-Marts than the dingy, cluttered Goodwills of the years past."

Canadian Business notes its "attention to customer preference is one of the keys to its success" in Canada, where it rides – and drives – a booming trend "as hordes of consumers, lured by a desire to stretch their household budgets, shun the pricier department stores...."

The Age, a major Australian newspaper, says of the small but growing chain in Melbourne that shopping there "is mandatory for your next dress-up do or wardrobe update. Every visit is like visiting a new store. It's a second-hand version of K-Mart and stock is updated daily...the eclectic mix of clothes is vetted to guarantee nothing shabby makes it out on the racks."

And readers' polls and critics'-choice articles and broadcasts across North America routinely name the company's outlets the best thrift stores in their cities. Both the *Las Vegas Review Journal* and its readers did recently, observing that the stores "have such an extensive selection, you actually can go in search of a particular item and have a reasonable chance of finding it. [They] also are organized by color and category, which makes shopping there akin to browsing a department store."

Over half a century, Savers and Value Village stores – now numbering two hundred – have become part of the fabric of their communities in three countries.

All this is Savers Inc., a network of two hundred Savers and Value Village stores operating in half of the American states and all ten Canadian provinces and gaining a beachhead in Australia. It's now owned jointly by Tom Ellison of Bellevue, Washington, and Berkshire Partners of Boston. Tom, as chairman, replaced himself as president and CEO with Ken Alterman, a corporate executive from the high-powered world of Pepsico Inc. who had been heavily involved in charities such as the Boys & Girls Club and the United Way.

But for most of the past half-century, this was a true family business with deep roots dating back to Tom's grandfather Ben and grand-uncle Orlo. During the Depression-devastated 1930s, they ran Salvation Army thrift shops throughout the western United States and a decade later left the Sally Ann to open their own privately run outlets. That heritage prompted Tom's father, William O. Ellison – Bill, or WOE to friends in the company – to launch his first store in 1954 and later to begin passing the business on by making sons Tom and Jeff and son-in-law John Bacon his active partners.

Another crucial partnership was the one he established from the start with non-profit charities, which collected used clothes and merchan-

Among the newest members of the two-hundred-outlet chain is this Savers store in Peoria, Arizona, which had its grand opening in September 2003.

dise for recycling and resale. Today this continuing collaboration is a vital propellant that fuels the programs of these organizations. Savers' presence in the market has also indirectly helped charities such as the Sally Ann and Goodwill Industries by modernizing the concept of the thrift store and making it a more respectable shopping destination for the mass of middle-class consumers.

While there's never been any doubt that Savers is operated as a private company, its very existence depends on working in lockstep with (at this writing) about 120 local branches of forty different charities. They run the gamut from regional non-profits such as Washington's Northwest Center for the mentally handicapped to national diabetes associations in Canada and Australia, from Big Brothers Big Sisters mentoring children to Bosom Buddies supporting women with breast cancer.

And if Savers Inc. is no longer strictly a family enterprise, it does try to retain the qualities that its founder built into the business. Its stores employ more than 8,500, many of them immigrant and entry-level workers who usually receive more than minimum wages and very welcome health coverage, matched retirement-savings contributions, and profit-sharing bonuses. These perks are all highly unusual in much of the retail-

Value Villages – located in parts of the western U.S., Alaska, and across Canada – have become synonymous with bargains and unexpected treasures.

ing universe, especially in the discount sector. Most of Savers' managers have come up through the ranks – only during periods of rapid growth are they hired from outside – and so there's always the possibility of working into much-higher-paid positions.

Management courses include extensive on-site training in any of twenty-five district stores and an intensive leadership-development program for high-potential managers. Annual retreats for managers and supervisors take them to warm oases in the winter, like Cancun and Maui, to celebrate their successes and plan for the next year at all-expense-paid events, which cost the company hundreds of thousands of dollars. All new employees complete an innovative computer program called JumpStart, designed in-house, which uses specific assignments to help them understand the business, the core values, and their own jobs – all at their own pace. Donna McMaster, who'd been marketing vice-president of the largest Australian department-store chain, joined the company in 2004 to run Savers Australia. After training for her position in the U.S., she remarked, "I loved JumpStart. I had never seen an orientation program like it."

THE CRITICS HAVE THEIR SAY

Not everyone views the company and its programs with wild enthusiasm or even simple kindness. On the Internet forum run by the International Workers of the World, disgruntled retail employees can complain about their working conditions, and some do about Savers and Value Village. Yet of the surprisingly few attempts to organize unions in the stores, only a handful have succeeded and all of the unionized locals failed within a short time. One case happened not long ago in Prince George, a city with a highly unionized workforce in the heartland of British Columbia, where the International Woodworkers of America organized about forty employees of a Value Village. But the union stopped bargaining with the company when it saw that the staff were no longer supporting its efforts. Ten months after union certification, the vote to decertify was an astonishing 100 per cent. In 2005 not a single store in the chain was unionized.

Other criticism has come from charities operating thrift shops that have to go head to head with the company's efficiently run outlets. Sometimes the competition is keen: for example, despite the presence of several Value Villages in Oregon, a chain of non-profit Goodwill stores there is highly successful, generating $58.13 million in a recent year – and earning its president $785,446 in salary and benefits. Sometimes not so keen: all Goodwill retail operations in British Columbia closed when they failed to compete during the 1990s. Dave Wunderlin, president of the Northwest Center in Seattle, says that when Savers' competitors approach him to work with them instead, they sometimes flash photos of Tom Ellison's gracious home on Lake Washington "and suggest these are evil people; they're exploiting you." Dave's reply: "We love these people."

But while both Goodwill and the Salvation Army occasionally bristle at their for-profit rival, they usually tend to take a live-and-let-live attitude. Major Gary Brown of the Sally Ann in Calgary, Alberta, told *Avenue Magazine* in 2004 that Value Village "do offer significant competition for us, but really our main challenge is that we've got too much [merchandise] to sort through sometimes."

From time to time, the media have also taken potshots at the company. They might point out that Savers is a money-making operation and its private owners profit from charitable donations – ("Charity for Billionaires," one headline said hyperbolically) – without noting that an operator of a non-profit Goodwill has personally reaped more than three-quarters of a million dollars a year. Mostly, journalists report the concerns of the local non-profit community when a Savers store opens in their area. In fact, the company's experience has been that, with some exceptions, contributions to non-profits actually rise when its advertising and solicitation prompt increased awareness about donating to charities and shopping in thrift stores. *Alberta Report* magazine noted in 1997 that Captain Don Grad of the Sally Ann in Calgary "does admit that Value Village's presence has made recycled clothing more acceptable, thus expanding the market."

Such rivalry appears to have re-energized the charities' own shops. In 1999, for instance, the Associated Press reported that Salvation Army and Goodwill stores in Ohio were upgrading – "shedding their reputation for being dingy and cluttered with castoffs. Some of the shops are moving uptown and getting a makeover." Five years later, a reporter on National Public Radio said, "Value Village and Savers have shown the thrift-store industry how to increase profits, and new thrift-shop chains are emulating the formula."

THE PEOPLE GIVE – AND TAKE AWAY

Savers' clientele embraces everyone from financially struggling college students and parents with young children to bargain-hunters, collectors, and shrewd shoppers of any age, income, and social stratum. As far back as 1992, the company was astutely defining its base of customers and their buying habits in terms that still hold true today:

> Savers and Value Village stores have a much larger radius of draw than most retailers. Customer surveys have shown that, in metropolitan areas, over half of the customers travel five miles or more to shop at the stores.
>
> While Savers and Value Village stores draw from a broad range of the demographic spectrum, the primary cus-

tomer base consists of middle-income families. These budget-conscious consumers are often ignored by most other retail thrift operations, which spend little time or money on customer service, store presentation or advertising.

Savers and Value Village stores also cater to a large number of senior citizens who choose to shop there not only for the low prices, but also for the items that they can find which are no longer manufactured or sold in regular retail stores. Many stores have a regular contingent of senior citizens who live nearby and shop there almost daily; all senior citizens are offered a 20 per cent discount on merchandise.

Teenagers and young adults are often frequent shoppers in search of unique clothing and accessories they cannot find in other stores.

With thousands of unique items arriving daily in every store, Savers and Value Village stores provide an entertaining and inexpensive shopping experience for customers who can usually afford to pay more, but choose to shop for bargains.

The buying habits of consumers in general have changed over the past few years. Today, they are more value-conscious than ever before, and are not always willing or able to pay regular department-store prices. They look for quality at the best price, yet may not be attracted to smaller, traditional thrift stores. They are also very interested in reducing waste by finding other functions for used products.

Savers' stores continue to offer consumers an ever-changing Everyman's and especially Everywoman's Marketplace of inexpensive if not ridiculously cheap recycled merchandise. The prime offering, of course, is women's used clothing and accessories in good condition, often with high-priced brand-name labels. But treasure-hunters come for castoff home and office furniture; second-hand books, videos, record albums, and CDs (sometimes sold on the Internet too); vintage jewelry, contemporary chachkas and bling, and assorted art and craftwork; housewares from tea cups to microwaves; and rare collectibles that may carry pricetags of hundreds or thousands of dollars yet still be considered a heckuva deal.

The donations can be surprising and sometimes downright bizarre. Jerry Hatfield, the chief executive officer of an insurance brokerage in Bothell, Washington, decided to downsize his collection of nearly five million sports cards in 2004 and looked for a worthy cause to receive 1.3 million of them. He chose Savers, which began selling sorted boxed sets of 3,000 football, baseball, basketball, and hockey cards at $9.99 a set; others were individually priced depending on their rarity. The proceeds were shared with three charities affiliated with four stores north of Seattle. Among those non-profits, fittingly enough, was the Moyer Foundation begun by Seattle Mariners pitcher Jamie Moyer and his wife to help "restore hope among children and families" through contributions to about a hundred organizations.

Some donations are made involuntarily. Currency totalling $10,952 turned up in a Sarnia, Ontario, store in a box of knee-high nylons (which also contained papers identifying the owner); $2,000 in a rolled-up sock in Houston, Texas; $1,500 in a stack of *Playboy* magazines that a boy's mother had confiscated (he got his money back). In early 2004 Christine Thorson, a pricer at a Value Village store in Surrey, B.C., found two diamond-encrusted solitaire rings in the pocket of a purse that had been donated to Canadian Diabetes. She took them to her supervisor and the jewelry was given to local police for investigation after being professionally evaluated at about $25,000. Following a year's attempts to find the gold rings' owner, the company auctioned them on eBay (starting at a low $9.99 apiece) – and fifty per cent of the $8,988 raised went to the charity. Two years earlier, the owner of another ring had been luckier after accidentally leaving her wedding ring in a purse she included in a bag of goodies for her Value Village in North Bay, Ontario. Realizing her mistake, Stacy Von Mierlo and her husband helped the store's staff sift through eight barrels of handbags – to no avail. But a month later, an employee found the wedding band and returned it to the wife.

The stories seem endless: A store in Salem, Oregon, received an artificial leg and arm; one in Seattle got a nineteenth-century memorial urn with the deceased's ashes inside (it was priced at $1,499.99); another in Kalua, Hawaii, had a pair of woman's underwear with a seventy-inch waist and a store in Regina, Saskatchewan, a business suit big enough for two employees to fit inside. Among the less-welcome donations have been a shrunken head in Spokane, Washington, and a bottled fetus in Portland, Oregon; a dead chicken, a pair of live cockatiels, and a loaded gun at a Value Village in Guelph, Ontario; and a hand grenade, mortar round, and miscellaneous ammunition recently left at another Village in Arlington, Washington – and promptly handed off to the police. Oh, and police also received the gram of cocaine worth $1,000 found in a coat in Kelowna, B.C., and a big garbage bag of leaves that a pricer in Ottawa, Ontario, thought was yard waste but turned out to be marijuana.

All these donations, even the oddest ones, represent recycling in its purest form – passing on the detritus, the discards of our acquisitive western societies, from one person, one family, one generation to another, who rescue and re-use it. The clothing, shoes, and such that don't survive Savers' rigorous winnowing process are also recycled (yes, for a profit) by baling and boxing them for resale to the developing world, including India and the nations of West Africa. Every year 220 million or more pounds of goods are shipped overseas to find new life instead of a final end in landfills.

VILLAGE JUNKIES, SAVERS SCREEN GEMS

No wonder then that in many parts of North America the company has become a bit of an icon, its name taking on near-legendary status among many shoppers. There is, however, the little matter of exactly what that name is. In the U.S. Pacific Northwest and across Canada, its stores bear the distinctive red-on-white signs of Value Village – except, that is, in the French-speaking province of Quebec, where they're called Village des Valeurs. In the rest of America and in Australia, the stores became Savers because some members of the extended Ellison family and others with no connection to the Bellevue company also operate what they call Value Vil-

Some clients of the Northwest Center, the Seattle-based charity for the mentally handicapped, work at the Value Village in Burien, Washington.

lages. (Which is why visitors to the Savers website see a pop-up message pointing out that such unaffiliated stores are found in Texas, Georgia, Virginia, Washington D.C., Minnesota, "and more that we may not be aware of.") If all this isn't confusing enough, the Savers name itself is open to misinterpretation: at a recent management retreat held in Nashville, amid the Bible Belt, the hotel thought the company was a religious organization and had booked one of its sessions in the Gospel Room.

In spite of the name game, budget-conscious consumers have no trouble finding the company's stores and regard them fondly enough to give them nicknames like "The VV Boutique" and simply "The Village." The brand has even entered the language as a handy means of comparison. One newspaper reporter writes that a local discount cinema complex is "like the Value Village of theaters; second-hand movies for dirt-cheap prices." Another describes a big-city communal sailing club: "This is the Value Village of the sailing world – most everyone can afford to join." A columnist describes how proceeds from a pop singer's fund-raising concert to help the poor in Mozambique stretched so far: "It's like the Value Village of philanthropy. You get huge bang for the buck."

It's that reputation for rock-bottom prices for decent goods conveniently displayed in a respectable environment that makes people passionate about Savers' stores. Sometimes too passionate, like the woman in London, Ontario (whose identity will not be revealed here) who confessed to Village employees that she'd actually had to seek therapy to help her refrain from shopping there so often. Exposing a less dramatic dependency, Jordan MacPherson, writing on a B.C.-based website called secondhand savvy, called herself a Village Junkie for her ingrained habit of rummaging through the stores once or twice every week. She was knowledgeable enough to list "ten secret shopping tips," which began with "Never pay more than at least half of what it would retail for. (The store pays for clothing per pound, not by brand name.)"

Jo Miller, the lead singer in what was a popular Seattle-based cowgirl band named Ranch Romance, once wrote a song titled "Village Idiot" that chronicled such devotion. Among its verses:

> She wore a glass stare, like she wasn't really there,
> She breathed in the air of pure desire,
> Movin' up and down the aisle, hummin' a tune
> Didn't know what she was lookin' for but knew she'd
>   find it soon.
> Hopin' that the prize would wear a special tag.
> She's just a Village idiot, it says so on her bag.
>
> There's value at The Village, the price is always right,
> No wonder you can find her shoppin' every single night.
> Can't seem to help, doesn't even try.
> Couldn't be a Village idiot without the urge to buy.
> She's waitin' for the manager's special after six,
> She's a bad junk junkie and she's needin' her fix.
>   (Copyright 1990)

Others find relief from stress in shopping thrift stores. Ann Rule, the former Seattle policewoman who writes bestselling true-crime books about serial killers such as Ted Bundy, describes her perfect day as sleeping in on an October morning, lunching with friends, and then wandering down to a Value Village – where fans have recognized her in astonishment and remarked on her presence there: "I thought you were doing so well."

For many loyalists, the thrift department stores have become an integral part of their lives, often marking their most important milestones. Perhaps that's why regular shopper Laurie Logan of Redwood City, California, wrote a will that in 1993 bequeathed all her clothing, household goods, and furniture to the local Savers store.

A happier occasion was a celebration of birth that four British-born women on Bowen Island, B.C., staged for a girlfriend during the early 1990s. They put a bindfold on Miriam Stewart and drove her to a Value Village in the Greater Vancouver city of New Westminster. She was such a devoted shopper there that her pals had arranged with the staff to have a table set in the front window of the store with fine linen, flowers, and candelabra. Then, blindfold off, they feasted on a catered Greek birthday luncheon. Angie McCulloch, one of the friends, recalls, "People peered in at these mad Brits dining deluxe right in the window of Value Village."

Another life-affirming event involved Ricky Beaudoin and Leah Simpson, faithful customers of the Kelowna Value Village store in the interior of British Columbia. They were nearing the check-out when he pulled a ring from a jacket pocket. Gazing into her eyes, he popped the question: "Leah, will you marry me?" They wed six months later. In Lubbock, Texas, Sharon Marshall spent two years planning her wedding and decided that nothing would be new – if it wasn't borrowed, it came from her local Savers store. That included vintage hat boxes, hats, and gloves adorning Victorian-style tables; silver serving pieces; and pretty displays of old books and candlesticks. Another bride, Tamara Macpherson of Kamloops, B.C., brought twenty female friends and family members to her Value Village on the very morning of her wedding day. She was treating the girls, aged seven to seventy-five, to a shopping spree, with the first stop the hat department.

A more satiric take on discount weddings was the ceremony that Amy Ellen Trefsger, a Seattle performance artist, indulged in not long ago. With the support of bridesmaids whom she dubbed matrons of art, she donned roller skates with pink wheels and literally tied a huge knot as she married herself in a park – her creative self, which she named

Artist Shamina Senaratine's installation piece for a Vancouver gallery made a social comment using traditional South Asian clothing from a local Village.

flatchestedmama. Her flowing white bridal gown came, of course, from Value Village.

Other artists and designers have plundered the company's stores for art supplies, props, and their own wardrobes. Across the border in Vancouver, Shamina Senaratine created an installation piece for an art gallery, which featured various traditional South Asian women's dresses she found in a Village costume section. Describing the theme of her work, she said, "What can we suppose about living in Vancouver in 2003, from the things offered for sale at the local Value Village? What I present is an expression of my desire to catalogue for posterity the experience of immigrants as they change in a changing Canada."

Jenifer Darbellay, an award-winning theatrical costume designer in Calgary, shops for herself in the city's Villages. Since her mid-teens, she has been clad in sequined shirts, leather jackets, and even workman's pants from their racks. "You've got to be well hydrated when you go in there," she cautions. "You've got to have patience; you've got to be a searcher." A prominent Toronto fashion stylist named Anya Shore also haunts the company's stores for personal bargains, like the Yves Saint Laurent blouse she discovered for two dollars. And on Earth Day 2005, the CultureJammers club at Seattle University hosted an Unfashion show in a tent, featuring student models in cool recycled clothing donated by Value Village stores.

Over the years, clothing from Savers outlets has surfaced on film and television. Men's suits showed up in *Driving Miss Daisy* with Morgan Freeman and Dan Aykroyd; suspenders and ties accessorized Paul Newman as Louisiana governor Earl Long in *Blaze*; and a peaches-and-cream cocktail dress with a cape graced Kim Basinger in *A Marrying Man*. Harry ("Judge Stone") Anderson's bizarre ties on TV's *Night Court* came fron the chain's stores, as did Robert ("Eldon") Pastorelli's gold lamé jacket on *Murphy Brown* (which also appeared in a cast photo of the show on the cover of *TV Guide*). A store itself was the backdrop for a thriller shot in Melbourne, which won the best-screenplay award at the Australian Film Awards. In *The Bank*, a farmer comes to the Brunswick Savers location in Melbourne to buy a suit for a court appearance.

FROM HOMETOWN HALLOWEENS TO MANHATTAN'S HIGH FASHION

For non-actors, the ultimate dress-up day in North America is Halloween, which in recent years has become Savers' and Value Village's Christmas-time. Their busiest season, beginning with back-to-school in August, now peaks in mid-October. Many of the hordes of Halloweeners visiting the store for the first time discover much more than masks and crazy costumes on the racks – and find themselves returning to stock their everyday wardrobes.

Even in the early days when Bill Ellison ran his stores, some shoppers in October picked up a fancy, outlandish, or dated dress or suit to don as party gear and found fun used clothes and props for their kids to disguise themselves for trick-or-treating. Then in the early 1990s, a feisty district manager in Canada, Mike Davison, realized the stores were missing a lucrative bet by not offering a broad selection of brand-new

Every fall Savers' stores explode with the Halloween Factory's displays of new seasonal merchandise, contests, face-painting, and even scary story-telling.

Halloween merchandise, from inexpensive costumes to home decor, to lure even more customers. His instinct was prescient: today the holiday competes with Christmas in overall retail spending, with more than $3 billion worth of sales during 2004 in the U.S. alone. And Savers' sales of new Halloween stock rose by twenty per cent that year over the previous October. By inventing a seasonal mascot called Dr. Frankenfrugal and using creative TV commercials with high production values, in-store costume co-ordinators as personal shoppers, and a special website for inspiration, the company has firmly positioned itself as the Halloween Superstore.

Paul Whitney, a columnist for the *Edmonton Sun*, in Alberta's capital, captured the spirit recently when he wrote: "OK, maybe I'm a bit of a Halloween purist. I only buy costumes items from Value Village. Some things are sacred. You go there, buy things for your costume, carefully seeking a bargain while shopping for green plaid blazers, wide purple ties, torn clothing, tuques and anything that resembles a Freddie Kruger hockey mask. This is stuff they cannot sell any other time of the year. Before Halloween they clear out tons of this stuff they don't want, and three days later it's all donated back. This is recycling at its best."

It may seem a stretch to go from being the reigning honchos of Halloween to leading a promotional assault on the high-fashion world of New York. But in 2004 the people of Savers did just that when they decided to take Manhattan by storm and raise the corporate profile in America's media capital. Their message was: "Revolutionize the way you

Manhattan's fashion editors were charmed by the Savers Showcase of fun and funky goods.

Featured were vintage furniture, offbeat fashions and housewares, and even a soapbox racer.

look at thrift shopping." They hired a local designer to style a "Savers Showroom!" with intriguing clothing, housewares, and furniture from the company's stores, including upscale merchandise from outlets on trendy Long Island. Then they invited editors from magazines that ranged from *Good Housekeeping* to *O the Oprah Magazine*, from *Esquire* to *Maxim*.

Three dozen of them showed up and seemed pleasantly surprised by the designer, funk, and vintage garb "for pennies on the dollar," the shabby chic furnishings "that don't break the bank," the D-I-Y décor "and customizable clothing," and the authentic Halloween costumes "without scary price tags." Janet Sobesky, lifestyle editor of *Woman's Day*, said, "You should have a store in Manhattan... New Yorkers live for this stuff." In the end, it was the little sisters of the major magazines that came through. *ELLEgirl*, in a photo spread of "the queen of the teens," credited Savers with a silver necklace the editors had picked up at the Showroom. *Seventeen* named Savers/Value Village as its favorite vintage shops (publishing the website address for store locations) and showed a pair of $6 cowboy boots from the promotion. And *CosmoGIRL* in its monthly calendar announced that five of its readers would win a $100 shopping spree at the chain. For a company that makes most of its revenue in the *schmatte* business – the Yiddish word for the rag trade, or used clothing – it was a sweet success.

Savers Inc. was now firmly ensconced in the twenty-first century, selling itself to a new market in a novel and imaginative way, setting the standard again for the entire thrift-store industry. But behind the glitz and glamor were the company's foot soldiers, battalions of men and women who endlessly gather the goods, laboriously sort and price them, and present them appealingly in the People's Store.

"Normally we have 500 OKs on hand."

TWO DAYS IN THE LIFE
CHAPTER ONE

On this warm, green St. Patrick's Day in the Pacific Northwest, Paula Keleci was plainly upset. The generally unflappable manager of Value Village in the Seattle suburb of Redmond, Washington, strode through the store's Back Room – the behind-the-scenes production department – in search of more used clothing for her employees to process. A local non-profit charity picks up donations from householders in the areas around well-to-do, white-collar Redmond ("Microsoft's backyard," as she explained), but it was updating its telephone-solicitation system. So for days its trucks had been maddeningly light on merchandise to deliver to the store. And this Thursday in March was the start of a regular fifty-per-cent-off sales weekend.

"Normally we have five hundred OKs on hand," Paula said, using the industry shorthand for a donation of goods equalling about 2.7 cubic feet, or two large grocery bags (and named for the "OK" that a charity's driver might check off when making a successful pickup from a donor). "Right now," Paula said, "my main concern is we're running out of product and I'm hoping something will show up here quick."

The compact forty-four-year-old – in jeans, rings on fingers and one thumb, big gold hoop earrings, a pair of sunglasses perched atop her long, raven hair – is a second-generation American, her family hailing from Spain. The people working the Back Room this morning – team members, in Savers parlance – were a meaty stew of nationalities from the Philippines, Mexico, India, and even a Russian-speaking young man from

Opposite: Paula Keleci, manager of Value Village in white-collar Redmond, Washington.

Azerbaijan. "Emil," Paula asked him, "do you have any clothes out there?" She pointed to the open-air loading bay at the rear of the store, where people drive up and drop off goods themselves at what's nicknamed an OSD – an on-site donation center.

"A little bit," Emil Gaybaliyev said in his hesitant English. You never know what you'll discover in an OSD. Recently a woman had left a native Indian basket, which Emil brought to Paula, wondering whether to throw it out. She recognized its museum quality, had some research done, priced it at $3,000, and the treasure sold within two weeks.

Now Paula hurried outdoors to comb through stacks of cardboard boxes facing banks of old furniture. No clothes worth processing. She looked at her watch: just before noon. "I'm going to call the charity," she announced. For her and other store managers, such inconsistencies of supply could soon be a problem of the past. Three stores in Phoenix were experimenting with a central depot that would receive and hold all the charities' donations in each city and then portion them out to each store in a steady stream each day. But for now, that was just a concept being road-tested and Paula desperately needed product.

At 12:20, just in time to feed the flow of goods, a white truck arrived, emblazoned with the non-profit's name, Community Services for the Blind (CSB), and the slogan "Your Donations Help Change Lives." The sixteen-foot-long step-van was laden to the top with castoff furniture, a rich miscellany of household goods – rugs, golf clubs, car seats, obsolescent typewriters, unloved pictures in frames – and what seemed like a small warehouse of clothing in boxes, green garbage bags and department-store shopping bags, some of them bearing classy labels like Nordstrom's.

Since seven A.M. the two drivers had clocked about sixty miles to make 142 pickups in Kirkland, a well-to-do lakeside community north-west of Redmond. "In early spring, just coming off the winter season, the donations go down so the number of calls we make has to go up," said Dan Spicer, a burly drivers' supervisor with eleven years' experience, who was on the route today with Bill Dye. "Our numbers should have been higher, but our new dialling system isn't functioning properly." Although many charities now use mailing cards to communicate with their donors, this one still connects with them by telephone ("because we don't want to

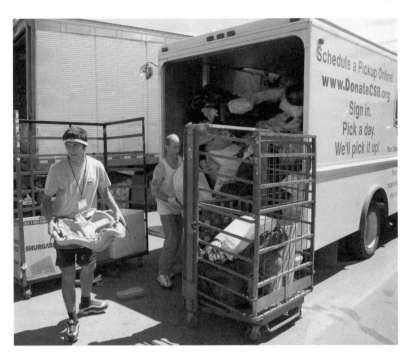

A truck from the Community Services for the Blind and Partially Sighted in Washington state discharges a brimming load of goods in Redmond.

lose that personal touch") or it encourages them to schedule their pickups online.

A solo CSB driver, working only four days a week in this physically demanding job, will accept a cornucopia of contributions, with some obvious exceptions ranging from old barbecues and building materials to toilets and waterbeds. Among the other no-nos are furniture he can't handle himself; food and cash donations; infants' equipment more than two years old ("there's a liability issue," Dan said); TVs and computer monitors (because broken ones can no longer be disposed of in local landfills); and anything that needs major repairing or cleaning. "But sometimes it's better to take it all rather than losing a donor."

The donors' bags can hold a Pandora's box of unwelcome surprises, like floor sweepings and chicken bones, even a live chicken once, the hide of a dog, and the blade of an unsheathed knife that stabbed a driver deeply in the back when he flung a bag over his shoulder. Then there are

Luci Jaspe began as a cashier at the Redmond store and is now an operations supervisor who regularly wins awards for her skill in overseeing co-workers.

the sex toys "and tons of Suzanne Somers ThighMasters – anything you see advertised on TV, within a year you see it donated."

In forty minutes the drivers had cleared their truck. Emil and the tall, tattooed, bushy-bearded head recycler, Ed Delvecchio, dumped some of the worst donations, including a battered table, directly into the maw of an outdoor compactor. It gets filled three times a week with unacceptable stuff that costs $9,000 a month in dumping fees. The truck that Dan and Bill had driven yielded seventy-five OKs of cloth, sixty-eight of "miscel" – miscellaneous merchandise, anything from fondue pots to outboard engines – and a good variety of furniture. The store had also credited them with sixty-five OKs from the on-site donation pool. While the charity receives less for these OSDs, it doesn't have to spend a cent or a second in collecting or handling them.

"Our drivers know they're raising money for the blind," Dan Spicer said. "Our used-merchandise division provides fifty per cent of what the organization makes. And I take pride in that." The Community Services for the Blind and Partially Sighted, to give its full name, is a United Way non-profit that offers free in-home services to people with severely impaired vision in three Washington counties. In a recent year, it had earned nearly $1 million in unrestricted funding from its collection program for Village stores.

"This is one of the best stores in this area – management is on top of everything," Dan confided. Underlining this accolade are the fact that Redmond is used as a training store for new employees and the honors on Paula Keleci's office walls: the lowest staff turnover in the whole company in 2003, the second-lowest in 2004; the award for operations supervisor of the year in '04 to Lucila Jaspe, who oversees the sales floor; and other citations for best furniture-pricing over several years to Amador Runez.

Once a carpenter in the Philippines, Amador at a wiry age sixty-four was still sorting and pricing up to 200 items a day in a jam-packed room: cabinets and couches, beds and mattresses, lamps and luggage, even the occasional doghouse. He tests radios and the TVs that OSD donors leave, lawn mowers, vacuum cleaners, bread machines, ice-cream makers, and anything else electrical. He also arranges the furnished goods in the store and after two weeks cuts the price, as he was doing this morning with a red grease pencil on a respectable wooden-and-cloth office chair that had dropped by $10 to a bargain $19.99.

In the Back Room, one of the twenty-three employees usually working there was sorting clothes piled in bags on carts from the three trucks that had arrived this afternoon. Mercedes Tanawan, a petite Filipino, had spent nearly eight years of eight-hour shifts with Value Village – "eight years at this table," she said, pointing at it emphatically. Each cart holds forty OKs and as a front-line sorter she can process seven carts a day. Mercedes was wearing a soft grey cap with a visor to keep dust off her hair, a blue corduroy jacket to save her arms from allergic reactions, but no gloves or a mask because they slow her down. "I'm not talking. I pay attention," she said with some pride. Describing the clothes and the little shockers that may accompany them, she said, "Sometimes it's good and sometimes it's caca from the baby." In the early days, the company used to dryclean better clothes, but the cost became prohibitive – and now it sells only those pieces of apparel that have evidently been cleaned or washed free of smoke, perfume, and mothball odors.

Retrieving goods from bags and boxes, Mercedes spread a sweater out, only to find stains on the front and under the arms. It went into the rag bin to her left, with the discards destined to become bales for recycling and bulk-sale to developing countries. A pair of men's jeans with a rip at the crotch followed. But the next pair, with a small hole, survived on the mound of acceptable goods accumulating to her right. They were vintage red-label Levi's, the best of which have been known to sell for $2,000 and more at some Villages (a quartet of Japanese regulars routinely pay up to $299 for them in Redmond and resell them in Japan for $600). Mercedes put all selected men's and women's clothing into one pile, to be separated by the "hanger" who works just to her right. Children's clothes went into another pile, shoes and books into boxes behind, and household fabrics, hats, belts into bins in front. Almost all stained items ended up in the rag bin, but a soiled garment of high quality might go down the line for pricing. Occasionally she held up something she admired, like a sheer black nightie with a Victoria's Secret label: "Very nice."

With all the OKs sorted, Mercedes took a tracking slip off the frame of the cart and put it in her pocket. Before lunch, she had finished four carts. When she was ready for another one, men on the floor pushed it in position so she could easily reach those endless bags and boxes.

Next to her, Pablena Aurelia separated the men's and ladies', draped them on hangers, and checked further for stains or tears. She placed the survivors on three "speed rails," like a dry-cleaner's tracks, and either she or a "stapler" attached tags to the garments. Partway down each rail, a pricer then wrote size and cost on the stapled tag – ranging usually between $1.99 and $9.99 (but with no $8.99 price point) – and pushed the garment down the line behind her. Melinda Torres, a ladies' pricer, gave each piece the fleetest of views, rejecting for spots under arms and in the crotch. She checked the pockets, did up buttons, tested zippers, looked for the size, estimated the price based on five criteria – quality, condition, wearability, rarity, and supply and demand. The entire transaction took about fifteen seconds per item. Melinda priced an unused Barishnikov exercise suit, still bearing an original $29.95 tag, at $7.99. A purple leather bomber jacket in nice shape except for a darkened collar went for $19.99, with Melinda shrugging as she wrote the price – maybe it was too high.

When a bunch of garments collected on a rack behind her, a supervisor arrived to help count and tally, recording the number of items at each price point. The tallies are entered into a computer and the results posted daily. The day before, Melinda's quota was to price 1,664 items at an average cost of $5.75. Instead she did 1,802 items at a $5.87 average (or $10,536 worth).

Finally, "racker-rollers" grouped the garments on rolling racks in the same order of size and color that they're displayed in the store, and took the racks, with about a hundred items apiece, on to the sales floor.

All of this – the physical task of sorting, the mental arts of pricing and tallying – had been done in the same way for decades. But even as the people in the production department worked ritualistically at the Redmond store, the company was field-testing new methods in other locations. Someday soon, the innovations could simplify the factory-like process by reducing the number of price points and introducing computerized touch-screens to cost and bar-code each item.

Elsewhere in the Back Room, Varsha Shah priced hard and soft toys, musical instruments, business supplies, silverware, glass, china, and collectibles of all kinds. "In India," she remarked, "they don't throw so much away." She has a shelf of books like *Miller's Antiques and Collectibles* and others to check on the value of dolls, silverware, patterned glass, and expensive Hummelware. Some days she sorts 800 items, tagging them with prices that will drop after a month on the floor. Special finds wind up in a glass showcase at the front of the store, like a golden trumpet for $149.99 and a signed 1993 handwoven Longaberger basket for $129.99. Pricers are encouraged to window-shop other stores, peruse catalogues, and even watch *Antiques Roadshow*.

Anything pricy Varsha will check with Paula – who at the moment was typically filling in for an ill worker by sorting footwear. Some pairs of shoes are cleaned before being sold, and others are mated with elastic bands and held for recycling overseas, especially soccer and tennis shoes. A team led by John Lawless, general manager of Savers' recycling operations in Fife, Washington, was visiting the store. His field managers were instructing the Redmond staff on which items can be sent to poor nations with tropical climates and primitive living conditions. So, for example, that means no winter boots, ice skates, roller blades, or fashionable high-heeled shoes, all of them useless in places like Sierra Leone. The question John and his people kept posing: "Are we recycling everything we can instead of having things go into the garbage?"

This afternoon, with the Back Room busy again, the sales floor was coming alive. Shoppers were massing for the fifty-per-cent-off weekend specials, marked by an orange tag, one of five different color codes. Blue-tagged items were the newest items on the racks and shelves this week and yellow ones the oldest, to be sold off for ninety-nine cents the following Monday after five weeks in the store. The red-vested figure of Luci Jaspe, the award-winning operations supervisor, could be seen patrolling the aisles, filling in as a cashier, rounding up shopping carts in the parking lot, cleaning up the dressing rooms, and noticing if there were too many garments stuffed in a rack. "This is unshoppable," she said at one point, calling for a "rag-off" employee to remove some of the overload in ladies' clothing.

Luci came to the Redmond store as a cashier eleven years earlier, fresh from the Philippines. Her warm manner shines through at the Sunday meetings she holds for her four cashiers. "I don't want them talking behind me. I make them all happy together, and if a problem arises, I talk to them, one-to-one, and we try to solve it."

One problem can be shoplifters, and the solution is often (as Paula Keleci says) "to customer-service them to death." Luci will make eye contact and acknowledge a light-fingered shopper by saying, "Ma'am, would you like to buy that coat? It looks so nice on you." Inevitably, the cowed thief-to-be agrees to purchase the item.

Roaming the store through the afternoon was Tony DiMaina, a still-sturdy bridge to the past. Nearly eighty years old, this little (Italian-American) leprechaun of a man was still feeling protective about Value Village and casting critical looks at the stores and the people running them today. He'd just returned from a retirement party for an employee at a nearby outlet who had started working for the company at the same time he had, thirty-three years ago. Moving from New York, where the only thrift stores were charity-owned and served the down-and-out, Tony had marvelled

Veteran manager Tony DiMaina

at the private business model that founder Bill Ellison created. "I thought Mr. Ellison was a genius," he said in an accent still marked by his Brooklyn boyhood.

Eventually he became manager of the Redmond store, which opened in 1984. As a seventy-two-year-old in 1997, he believed he was ending his career there (with Paula as his production supervisor) but was lured out of retirement to work every other day as a miscel pricer at the Village in Renton, Washington. Softer on shoplifters than some managers, he told the story of releasing one culprit after a gentle but firm talking-to. The man returned later to explain he had a daughter just going to college – "and he wanted to say thanks for speaking to him that way instead of calling the police and ruining his life and hers."

(Some thieves can be astonishingly stupid: a man stole a pair of pants worth $14.99 from a Village in Milwaukie, Oregon, and left the price tag and his old pants in the change room with $19 in the pocket.)

There were no shoplifters being targeted this Thursday, just the occasional customer with eyes glazed by the scope of choice in the 17,500-square-foot store in central Redmond (population 45,000-plus). It sprawls in a small, pleasant strip mall of 1960s vintage owned by Tom Ellison, heir to the Savers Inc. legacy. Value Village, announced by its bold sign, is sandwiched between a deli and a beauty salon; a Kinko's anchors the far end of the mall. Inside, signs high on the walls say *Welcome to America's Favorite Thrift Store, Complete Outfits for under $20, and Exchanges Gladly Accepted* (a customer service the company pioneered in the thrift industry). The various departments in the brightly lit interior have their own graphically pleasing signs.

Kevin, an unemployed roofer, had already found a $49.99 eight-drawer oak jewelry cabinet for his wife and now was looking in the miscellaneous housewares department for a signed cobalt-blue plate – like the one a buddy had bought here for $40 and resold at auction on e-Bay for $1,800. All Kevin came up with was a cast-iron pan.

June, a silver-haired Englishwoman in a denim jacket, is a more successful Value Village habitué, as she demonstrated by displaying a business checkbook recording line after line of payments to the store over the years. She and her husband hunt here constantly for antique toys and Paddington bears to stock a little shop they have outside Redmond. "This is the best hobby I've ever had," she said. "My clothes all come from here. I'm the original Second Hand Rose. I clothed all my grandchildren here until they got old and too fussy."

Patti, a tall blonde with a wide smile, was visiting her mother from the east coast. Together they were making one of their regular safaris through the store, along with Patti's three-year-old son. "As far as kids' clothes, they go through the pre-school stage so fast and an outfit here can look brand-new," she said. Her sister has five children and all their clothes came from the Village. Her mom, Mary, said, "I've come in here and found things for them like this" – an as-new red vest for $2.99. For herself, Patti found a Pooh-Bear sweatshirt (fifty-per-cent off at $6.99) and for Mary a floral fleecy cotton sweater for gardening ($2.99).

The store averages sales of $17 per customer, among the highest in Savers' American chain. As Paula Keleci pointed out, "There's a lot of money in this area" – what with Microsoft and other computer-software companies, research and development industries, and diverse manufacturers. Late on St. Patrick's Day, Paula was spending some rare time in her office, still upset about the relatively few OKs the store received from three truckloads of goods. "I get in trouble with my district manager a lot for not doing my office stuff," she said. "Sometimes I cannot wait to get to work in the morning. I wonder how much we made yesterday.... My priority is driving my supervisors to make their goals so we can make our profit goals every month. Over the years I've hired so many people who have never had a job before, and to see them excel and challenge themselves has been so rewarding to me." She was sounding like a corporate commercial.

Employees as well as managers can share in the profits they generate. Newcomers in the Back Room and on the sales floor start here at above minimum wage, but for many of them – especially immigrants in a country without universal health care – the prospect of a generous medical and dental plan is almost more important. After three months, the staff can join the plan as well as have a week's vacation and forty-eight hours' sick time. Beyond that, they're eligible for profit-sharing contributions of about 1.1 per cent of their annual earnings. If they put a percentage of their pay into a 401-K retirement savings plan, the company will match the amount. And, as an additional, much-valued enticement, they can buy store clothing for fifty per cent off and other merchandise for smaller discounts.

"We've doubled the profit in five years," Paula said. "A lot of that has to do with our process. When I came here, we did twelve hundred OKs a week and now we do two thousand. The month of March is typically low in donations. After Christmas we get just tons of stuff – all the broken toys – and the spring and summer are crazy as people are cleaning out. And in October" – the Halloween season – "we'll be as high as 2,200 OKs. In October last year, we were in the top three or four stores in the country."

A VILLAGE IN VICTORIA

On this sea-scented, sun-kissed day just before Halloween on the west coast of Canada, Brenda Beecroft was plainly pleased. The gregarious manager of Value Village in Victoria, the capital of British Columbia, was making one of her frequent high-profile sweeps through the store. She wanted to keep staff morale humming as she viewed the state of the sales floor ("Someone needs to clean up women's shoes and the pictures wall") and noted the levels of stock in the Back Room. There was an ample supply of OKs arriving from her charities, Canadian Diabetes and Big Brothers Big Sisters of Victoria, collected from homeowners and their strategically placed drop boxes. And Brenda was anticipating a busy day with customers who'd received their government Family Allowance checks – not to mention all those ubiquitous Halloween shoppers.

Like Redmond, Victoria attracts numerous high-tech companies, but it also has sizable populations of well-paid government employees conducting the province's business and prosperous seniors from across Canada lured by the salubrious climate of the warmest major city in the nation. The weather and the quaint and sometimes kitschy ambience of the largest center on Vancouver Island make it a tourist mecca, and in summer even some of the crews and passengers from Alaska-bound cruise ships stop in at the Victoria store. B.C. is one big film location and recently the designers of the new *Charlie's Angels* movie had found some of their props and clothing here to reflect a '70s look.

Opened in 1988 within a former flea market, it's the largest outlet in the Savers world, twice the size of Redmond's at 35,000 square feet
and with more than twice the roll of employees, up to ninety full- and
part-time, many of them university students. (Unlike Redmond, Victoria
has a large number of transients among its 775,000-plus population and
twenty-five of the staff had been working here three months or less.) The
production department – the length of a football field – can process about
13,000 items or more a day for sale in the store.

Brenda had been up since 5 A.M. tending to her toddler son before
coming to work. Throughout the day, she spent little time in her peach-
colored office with its faded seascape prints. At a mature thirty-two, she'd
been working for the company for fifteen years, starting as a part-time
cashier in Maple Ridge, B.C.. Within six months of becoming a production supervisor at a Village in Burnaby, another Greater Vancouver munic-
ipality, she was made manager – at twenty-one – and helped turn the
money-losing outlet into one of the top ten most-profitable stores in
Canada. "I had a really great staff; I really care about my staff," she
recalled, her pale-blue eyes watering ("I don't cry very often"). For the
past two years, she'd been running the Victoria location and supervising managers in Nanaimo on Vancouver Island and Prince George on the
mainland – a store she had launched with the best sales figures of any
opening in the company's history

During the past week in Victoria, she'd stapled tags on clothing with a pricer who was a bit behind and spent a couple of hours as a
cashier on a hectic Saturday – to constantly communicate with her team
members, ask for their ideas, mother new employees who looked a little
lost. Sounding like some dream manager out of a motivational textbook,
as Paula had in Redmond, Brenda said, "Every day I wake up and look
forward to coming to work. I enjoy the people and the problem-solving."

Full-time Canadian staff have a deferred profit-sharing plan
amounting to 3.5 per cent of their gross salary and a registered retirement savings plan in which the company contributes twenty-five cents
for every employee dollar. In a country with basic universal health care,
Savers offers an extended plan covering prescriptions, dental work for
the whole family, and a family assistance program for short-term coun-
selling. Vacation time runs from two weeks after a year to four after ten

Brenda Beecroft's organizational abilities and her tact in supervising staff in Victoria have led her to a new post of Greater Vancouver's district manager.

years and an annual extra floating day off. A Christmas bonus based on position and length of service varies from less than a hundred dollars to a few thousand.

There can be modest monthly cash incentives too. This morning Donna Hunter, a small dynamo with sixteen years' experience, was one of four pricers in the Back Room, each generating up to 550 items a day. Donna was working in the bed and bath department, which can range from antique doilies to purses to soft-goods clothing accessories. "We've always been number-one [in production for Value Villages]," she said. "We were $100,000 over our quota last year." Pricers can earn a bonus of $75 a month for meeting their goals.

Sometimes their work results in strange surprises – such as a wriggling burlap sack. As Donna tells the story: "The worst was a huge live python snake, about six to eight feet long, that someone in the miscel department found. She thought it was a rubber snake until it turned its head. She threw it at me and I flung it." Safely back in the sack, it was sent straight to the SPCA where, by sheer chance, the son of the store's

Inge Brosius brings an expert's eye, based on long expeirence, to her specialized work as a pricer of jewelry, antiques, and other collectibles in Victoria.

then-manager – a woman terrified of snakes – bought the python and brought it home.

For the odd employee, the routine of pricing can produce psychological effects as well. Sheri Belrose, a young woman who had been costing kids' clothing for three years, said, "I have recurring dreams about Value Village: we go mountain-climbing and we lift up rocks and find clothes and the next corner we turn, we have to price all of them."

Inge Brosius is an older pricer who has been evaluating antiques and collectibles for eleven years in Victoria, where relatives from the Prairie provinces routinely arrive to clean out the estates of deceased seniors: "This store give you a sense of what society is like – that it's the disposable society. People have to work so hard for everything and yet they have to have the latest of everything. And sometimes I get emotional: who passed away? You spend your life working for something and what happens? It ends up here."

As she spoke, Inge was examining items through a jeweler's glass and putting price tags on necklaces, earrings, watches, special pieces to go in a locked showcase, and others to be displayed as possible Christmas gifts. She studied the stones on a pinkie ring: "They could be zirconia. They're too dull to be diamonds. I'll take a chance that they are zirconia and the gold is 10K." She marked the ring at $39. She also prepares bags for people who make jewelry ($4.99 a bag) and small gold items with carat markings that jewelers buy to melt down for the metal ($39-$49). Older women like to buy bags of several pairs of earrings for $1.99. Inge began work on a three-pound bag of watches she'd set aside: a lady's Gruen at $38, another at $3.99 because it needed a battery and there was no way of knowing whether it would run. Watches in rough shape are bunched for sale to dealers who want the straps.

She was processing about 200 articles in two hours, from Dresden figurines to vintage Christmas decorations. Among her jewelry finds was a necklace of huge pearls, which sold for about $600. She knew they were real – "you grit them," she explained, by rubbing them between your teeth; the authentic ones feel like sand. Some expensive-looking gems and timepieces might go to a jeweler for appraisal. A diamond-encircled watch with a heart-shaped face, found in a purse, was appraised at $1,235, priced in the store at $300, and bought for half that in a December sale. The best things end up at antique auctions, where they can fetch good prices, even after auctioneers take their share. A cartoon cel – a celluloid frame from an animated film – fetched $7,500 at a local auction not long ago.

The libraries of all the Canadian seniors who die in Victoria yield enough volumes to help make the local Village the top book-sales branch in the company. "We're so lucky because we get so many antiques and old books," said Stephanie Smillie, who was handling the store's books, magazines, videos, and music albums and CDs. A twenty-nine-year-old bibliophile in spite of her punk appearance, complete with a spiked collar, she'd worked in new and used bookstores and was currently enjoying one of the two Jane Austen books she hadn't yet read. From a tower of books cascading around her, she pulled a Bible from 1862 with wonderful line illustrations, which she priced at $89. First editions by well-known authors or signed books usually go into a showcase on the sales floor. This afternoon it also held *Great Men and Famous Women*, published in 1894 with pen-and-pencil sketches, and a 1970 edition of *My Crowd* by the bizarre cartoonist Charles Addams, going for $159.99.

(When the store in Guelph, Ontario, found a book called *A Star's Progress*, written under a pen name by the famous author Gore Vidal, book pricer Karen Dietz saw that it was selling for $7,000 Canadian on the Internet. Her copy was priced at $4,000 for sale by Dutch auction – with the figure dropping by $50 daily – and it sold for $700.)

Working toward her 1,200-item daily quota, Stephanie was quick to discard all *Reader's Digest* condensed books "because there are so many of them." None of the men's magazines survived either because the periodical racks are near the children's area. Videos taped off television programs went into the garbage bin. Evaluating vinyl albums, she consulted the *Official Price Guide to Records*; the Beatles' original *Hard Day's Night* and *Magical Mystery Tour* were each tagged at $125. Stephanie once treated herself to a Marlene Dietrich album, which she plays at bathtime "because it feels so decadent."

Ordinary records cost $1.49, videos $2.99, audiotapes 99 cents, and books from 69 cents to $3.99, sorted under headings like biographies, true crime, and vintage/collectibles.

The store verges on Chinatown, a block from historic Fan Tan Alley, in an area that's slowly being tarted up. But though a design academy and a home-furnishing shop are neighbors next door, it's flanked by two homeless shelters for street people and, around the corner, a Sally Ann hostel. "Last night we had a junkie who had to be removed by the police," Brenda Beecroft said. The man tried to demand $50 back for an old CD player he hadn't bought there, and when the manager asked how she could help, he invaded the staff area and eventually smashed the stereo before being arrested.

Some of the staff out front the next afternoon were wearing Halloween accessories, including devils' horns. Teenagers were buying new costumes: the Bleeding Grim Reaper, a seven-piece animated suit, and the "classic" Unknown Phantom ("Easy to see out! No one can see in!"). Ten-year-old Whitney was putting together a Cleopatra outfit: "We're studying Egypt for school," she said. On a special Halloween Day, the store had 1,600 customers, most of them parents with kids getting their faces painted, listening to scary stories, wrapping themselves like mummies in toilet paper, and winning prizes at the bottom of a bucket of spaghetti "brains." By mid-October, the space allotted to ghosts-and-goblins goods had shrunk, and team members were starting to put out some of the thousand boxes of Christmas items gathered over the year.

The sales-floor staff were awaiting a regular visit from a genteel elderly woman, her hair in a bun, who lived in a posh area of town: "She comes in almost every day at four o'clock with a daughter looking for those finer things – pictures, lamps, jewelry," Brenda noted. Meanwhile, a middle-aged divorcée named Sarah had bought a red leather jacket in splendid condition for $7.99 and a set of sheets, pillowcases, and a duvet cover for $30. "I've found a nice top here for $9.99 for a job interview and then got the part-time contract working for a non-profit," she confided. "Even when my financial circumstances were better, I still came down here. I've seen people who were dripping money. My whole house is furnished by Value Village. Also, I don't get hassled by salespeople; I can spend hours and hours here all on my own." She'd already spent three and a half hours shopping. On a recent sale day a husband and a wife had spent less time and about $1,000 filling five shopping carts to furnish their new bed-and-breakfast.

Observing all this frugal yet fervent consuming, the ghosts of Ben and Orlo Ellison might have looked on in wonder, if not sheer puzzlement. Their Salvation Army selves of the 1930s would find it hard to believe the boggling variety and quality of goods gathered here from around the world. Their entrepreneurial spirits, which they set free in the 1940s with their own stores, would marvel at their descendants' evolution of the business model they had begun so long ago.

"Dad was a man of tremendous generosity."

ROOTS AND BRANCHES
CHAPTER TWO

They were the Fix-It Men of the Salvation Army in the far west of America during the Dirty Thirties.

Benjamin Ellison and his brother Orlo were budding entrepreneurs who soldiered on faithfully over nearly three decades for the British-born religious organization. The Sally Ann, as it came to be fondly called, had a military cast – ordinary members as soldiers, their leader a general – and a mission to help society's least fortunate in the most practical ways, by offering them food and clothing, basic shelter and honest work. The Ellisons, descendants of a Scots-Irish immigrant family, were organizers and trouble-shooters for a string of the Army's thrift stores. They sold cast-off clothes and a hodgepodge of miscellaneous merchandise through the booming 1920s, the Depression-ridden '30s, and the war-torn '40s.

Today there are as many as thirty million Scots-Irish in the U.S., whose forefathers arrived in a mass immigration of about 400,000 from northern Ireland during the eighteenth century. They formed forty per cent of the Revolutionary Army and most of the Confederate troops in the Civil War, with many of them also serving on the Union side. Modern American warriors of that heritage include General George S. Patton and Audie Murphy, the most-decorated soldier of World War II and later a popular actor. Among other Hollywood stars of Scots-Irish descent have been Ava Gardner, John Wayne, and Robert Redford. Out of the same ethnic pool sprang a dozen or so presidents, from Andrew Jackson and Ulysses S. Grant to Ronald Reagan (on his mother's side) and Bill Clinton.

Opposite: Esther and Ben Ellison, in their Salvation Army garb, with sons Herb and Bill.

And extraordinary American writers, including Mark Twain, Edgar Allan Poe, and Margaret Mitchell, author of *Gone With the Wind*.

James Webb, who wrote about his own ancestry in *Born Fighting: How the Scots-Irish Shaped America*, notes: "They are naturally rebellious, often impossible to control.... They are filled with wanderlust, but no matter how far they roam, their passion for family travels with them. Underlying these seeming contradictions is a strong unwritten code of personal honor and individual accountability.... The Scots-Irish are a fiercely independent, individualist people."

Among them were the extensive Ellison clan, and among the present-day Ellisons are Bill and his brother, Herb. Dr. Herbert J. Ellison, as he's more formally known in academic circles, is one of North America's leading experts on the history and politics of Russia and the international relations of East Asia. One of his many roles is professor of Russian history and international studies at the Henry M. Jackson School of International Studies and the history department at the University of Washington. (In 2005 the university established an endowed Herbert J. Ellison Center for Russian, East European and Central Asian Studies – "much of the generous endowment capital," Herb says, "was provided by my brother Bill, my nephew Tom, and by many of my numerous cousins.) `

As a professional historian, he's fascinated by his own past. In an essay he prepared for a recent family reunion in Manchester, Ohio, Herb Ellison sketched the background of his people as far back as 1610. That's when James I, the king of England and the son of Mary Queen of Scots, undertook the first major movement of Scottish Protestant farmers to northern Ireland as a counterbalance to the defiant Irish Catholics.

Over the next century the transplanted Scots faced fierce opposition from the Irish – especially after political and religious strife in England under the pro-Catholic James II prompted continuing attacks on the Presbyterian church in Scotland and Ireland. More damaging were the trade restrictions and the usurious increases in farmland rentals the English imposed on Ireland. In the 1700s the Scots Irish began emigrating to what they hoped were the safer circumstances of the New World. But there they met harrowing conditions too; fortunately, they were a tough breed of people, as Herb Ellison writes:

For the many unable to afford the cost of passage the only way to secure it was to arrange an indenture contract in America, either in advance or on arrival in America where the shipmasters would not permit debarkation until they were paid. The courage with which these people endured dangerous and difficult crossings and the challenge of finding a livelihood is awesome, as is the speed with which they adjusted to their new lives in America, both on farms and in the cities, and as a major group in the settlement of the frontier.

The Scotch Irish played a major role in the settlement of the American West. They comprised a large share of the frontier land settlement and became involved in the struggle against both the French and the Indians in the French and Indian War of 1756-63. They were among the earliest settlers to enter the Ohio Valley territory ceded to the English by the French at the end of the war, and their participation in frontier settlement extended across the mountains after the War of Independence into Pennsylvania, Kentucky and Tennessee, as well as Ohio. They proved themselves remarkably adept at dealing with the constant threat of Indian raids, adopting the dress and the fighting tactics of the Indians for their own defense, even as they adopted many of the Indian food crops and knowledge of animal life in the frontier regions....

To what can one attribute the impressive success of the Scotch Irish in confronting the formidable challenges of their life in Ireland, the daring venture in the crossing to America, and the courageous way in which they met the challenge of building a new life in America, often as the advance wave of American frontier expansion and settlement under extremely difficult conditions?

Much of the reason is evident from their ability to cope with the harsh challenges of life in Ireland for more than a century before beginning the migration to America. They had a well-deserved reputation as hard workers, fierce warriors and pious Christians who built solid agricultural and commercial communities, valued education and resisted all encroachments upon their religious and personal freedom.

OLD VALUES IN A NEW WORLD

Among the hard-working, courageous emigrants was John Ellison, born in 1730 in County Tyrone, who brought his family to America just eleven years after it declared independence from England in 1776. He had four sons and a daughter. At least two of the boys had to demonstrate immense courage during their lives. The third son, Andrew, settled in the southern Ohio river port of Manchester, but in 1793 was captured by Shawnee Indians and held for six months. After forcing him to run a gauntlet – two rows of men armed with clubs to strike him – they took Andrew to Detroit and traded him for a blanket from an Englishman, who released him to return home on foot. The fourth son was Robert, who was married to Rebecca Lockhart in Ireland in 1802 before coming to the U.S. and serving in the War of 1812 against British and Canadian forces. Robert sired five daughters and five sons, including Moses. One of Moses's seven children was middle son William, whose family of four included Anthony Titus, born in 1868, who married Ita Florence Nash, eight years his younger. Titus, as he was called, broke from his father over a disagreement and eventually homesteaded in eastern Montana.

And it was Titus and Ita who, like Robert and Rebecca, produced five more female Ellisons and five males – among them Benjamin, born in Piqua, Kansas, in 1895, and Orlo, born a year later. Today, Ben's son Herb recalls his grandparents as remarkable people. "Ita was highly intelligent. I adored that woman. She was remarkable because she bore these ten children on this dry farm in Montana under enormously difficult circumstances. And she was an avid reader and a very good conversationalist

Sally Ann stalwarts Ben and Esther Ellison

– and a goldmine of history of the family. We went to see her every summer. She believed in having a big old house with lots of room for all the in-laws. Ita died in 1967 and was still quite lucid. I went back to visit her three years before that and she was still driving and scared the dickens out of me because she still had not managed the clutch.

"Titus taught school in Montana and wrote quite actively. My father once took me to a historical archive and library to see things his father had written on stock-raising. They had terribly dry years and my father's youngest brother, Uncle John, told me about winters when the only thing that they had to eat was the vegetables. They didn't have enough animals and feed for them, so they would just eat a mix of peas, carrots, and whatever else in a cream sauce." While the girls slept in a three-room log cabin, the boys bunked down in a barn, even during thirty-below weather.

Titus died when he was only fifty. The day before his death, he'd told his eldest son, Ben, that he wasn't going to be around forever and wanted him to be the head of the family. Ben was twenty-four and while he tried to keep the family together, relatives had to take some of his nine siblings in. His much-younger brother John would someday name one of his own sons for him, the most remarkable man he ever knew.

Herb's brother, Bill, says that their father held many jobs in Montana: "He worked on a railroad, he worked at farming, herding cattle – anything he could do to survive. His brother Orlo, fifteen months younger, met a girl named Stella in Helena, Montana, who was a member of the Salvation Army and she invited him to church with her. He in turn told Ben about it and Stella had a friend, Esther. And that's how my mother and father got together."

Ruth Esther Anderson's father was a building contractor specializing in decorative stonework, who came to Helena to erect a wing of the state capital building. Later, with the boom ebbing in the mining and agricultural town, he took a contract in Peru, where he died of a fever, leaving his wife with six children. Luckily, Esther's mother, from a Swedish commercial family, was very entrepreneurial and opened a tobacco and news shop in downtown Helena. Esther worked there as a child. Because her mom was well educated, speaking four languages as did most Swedes of the day, she insisted that her girls be too. All but one daughter, who ran off with an Irish preacher, went on to higher education. Esther had attended teachers' college in Great Falls, Montana, and was now teaching in the Helena area. Raised under the rather dour strictures of a Swedish Lutheran, she was introduced to the warmth and enthusiasm of the Sally Ann, where she played piano and sang with her sweet voice during services, and soon decided to join the Army.

Family legend has it that by now Ben had fallen in love with Esther and she influenced his decision to become an Army officer as well. Whatever the truth of that, he did become a probationary captain in 1922 out of the Billings, Montana, corps and attended the Sally Ann's western training school with her in San Francisco. Over the next five years, according to the Army's records, he served in Butte and Havre, Montana, and Richmond, California, sometimes doing public-relations and fundraising tasks. Ben and Esther married in 1927 and a year later had their first child, William Oliver, in Eugene, Oregon. This was Bill, who was destined to follow in the footsteps of his visionary, caring parents. Herbert and Beverly followed in the next three years as the church moved their folks to Portland, Oregon, and Boise, Idaho.

In 1929 the stock market crashed, precipitating the Great Depression of the 1930s. At its peak, sixteen million Americans – a third of the workforce – were unemployed and in need of the simple basics of food and shelter. Early in the decade, the young family was in Aberdeen, Washington, where Ben was promoted to adjutant. "Father was overseeing bread and soup lines," Bill says today, "and when I was four or five years old I went with him and saw 200 men in a line waiting with tin cups to be fed."

Herb recalls that "Dad saw the worst of the Depression from Washington state. It made such a vivid impression on me when he went up to the coast to load a truck with fish and I watched all these salmon being dumped into the truck bed to feed people. The Army had some links with the state welfare department. The state cooperated with them and provided some of the funds and regarded them as a useful adjunct."

"Until the later years, we were never really established in one place," Bill says. "It was wherever there was a fire to put out. That's because Dad and Orlo were now becoming the premier operators of the thrift stores for the Army. They were so successful that when a store would start failing, one of them would be transferred to that location."

In 1934 the Ellisons moved on to San Jose, California, and within a year went southeast to Fresno as Ben began work with the legendary men's social service department. There was some irony in the service he offered the many men whose drinking had led them to financial ruin, family strife, and finally to the shelters of the Sally Ann. Despite

The Army's American thrift stores during the booming 1920s and the depressed 1930s were a grab-bag of salvaged goods displayed in bins and barrels.

the church's prohibition against alcohol, both Ben and his wife, Esther, were secret drinkers. His liking for bourbon didn't seem to affect his role in the church or his relations with the extended family. "He was really an old Montana cowboy who had a really tough life," Bill says. "He functioned, but he had an addiction problem." But it wasn't until the end of his life that Ben would admit that he was an alcoholic.

MARCHING THROUGH THE WEST

The Salvation Army had its birth in the good works of a Methodist minister, William Booth, who started the Christian Revival Society in the England of the mid-1860s. Along with preaching the gospel to the under-privileged, he and his feminist-leaning wife, Catherine, offered them basic learning, soup kitchens, and relief aid. By 1878 the organization had evolved into the Salvation Army, complete with military ranks and uniforms. And two years later the Army was marching into America. Within a decade it had opened a Cheap Food and Shelter Depot for the drunk and the homeless – the beginning of its men's social service centers. Near the end of the century, salvage brigades of indigent men in New Jersey and New York were housed and fed in dormitories and employed to collect paper, rags, and miscellaneous goods in pushcarts and repair them for resale – in the stores of what were now being called industrial homes. A history of the Army called *Marching to Glory* remarks, "The idea of collecting old clothes and discards, hiring the poor to repair them, and then selling the improved results to other needy persons was not original with the Army, but the Army was the first agency to employ it on a large scale and to bring it to public attention."

During the early years of the Depression, the Sally Ann's resources were severely strained: "The financial circumstances of the industrial homes grew daily more desperate, as funds from every source evaporated and expenses multiplied. Social officers regarded it as a 'nightmare'; there were days in which there was no food of any sort to offer the desperate men, and no money to pay them even the twenty-five cents a week over their board they had been promised for their labor."

By the mid-'30s conditions had improved slightly and men's social services, in which Ben and Orlo were involved, were now able to cope with the crisis more efficiently. The Army had long since been using trucks to gather goods door to door, often prompted by a homeowner's telephone call or postcard. Their retail stores, which had once been ramshackle and jammed with junk, were starting to be slightly modernized with clear pricing, racks to hang some of the clothes, and antique objects centralized in their own section to attract dealers and collectors. *Somebody's Brother*, a history of the Sally Ann's social service department, observes, "Officers in the West were apparently the first to use modern equipment, such as compressed-air painting and large cleaning vats and woodworking machinery, in order to clean and repair furniture for resale."

Ben and Orlo Ellison fit into that western ethos as social entrepreneurs who became two of the key organizers, and re-organizers, of the Army's shops. George Duplain – who became a major in the Sally Ann and the author of an operations manual for its thrift shops – later described the Ellisons as "nice guys, Orlo especially. Orlo was a very astute, very clever businessman [who] would have become one of the top leaders in the Salvation Army." Orlo, who married Stella, had followed his older brother into the organization; between 1935 and 1949 he served with the social service department in Seattle, San Francisco, Long Beach, California, and Denver, Colorado. Orlo is credited with developing the idea of putting color-coded tags on merchandise to track salvage inventory. According to family history passed on to the current generation, it was Stella who first came up with the name "thrift stores." Esther, meanwhile, was not only mothering three kids but also working in the stores, having developed strong organizational skills serving in her mother's shop in Helena.

Both Herb and Bill have memories of the stores in the Denver area, where the mobile family moved in 1936. The Depression had left one out of every four of the city's adults jobless. President Franklin D. Roosevelt's New Deal created the WPA, the Works Progress Administration, which spent more than $42 million in Colorado trying to put people back to work on civic projects. Ben and Esther began organizing thrift shops throughout the state.

"The Depression really didn't end until World War II," Herb says, "and as a kid later on in the '30s I would go down to the men's social service center and some really nice guys working there taught me things about electricity and woodwork. They were clients, men with no other jobs who got work there for very modest salaries. They'd converted a big hotel structure and it had a large dining area. . . .

"Dad was a man of tremendous warmth and generosity. He loved entertaining and we always had a full house on weekends. He brought home some of the more interesting people in the social service center. One of them Bill and I remember fondly was John Kerr Mitchell, an Oxford graduate who came to America with Lever Brothers Soap. Mitch, as we called him, had alcohol problems, but he was a well-educated man and I had very interesting conversations with him about what Oxford was like. He took care of us kids when the folks would be away in San Francisco for meetings.

"The corps operated a big Sunday school with masses of kids who would pack a bus in this poor area in Denver. We got to know a lot of the kids and some of them became very good friends over the years. There was also a camp at Palmer Lake, near Colorado Springs – marvelous in

*Ben and Orlo Ellison helped rescue failing Sally Ann thrift stores in the western U.S.,
which were usually linked with men's social centers like this one.*

the summer. The Army did a tremendous amount for kids in those years.
I never will forget going with Dad one Sunday to a place where they had
caught a couple of Hispanic youngsters who were thieving from the so-
called serving room for the stores. They were going to charge the kids and
wanted his authorization. He said, 'I would prefer that you would release
them to me' – and they did. He told the boys he could provide them with
work for money. That was the way that he was and the way that an awful
lot of those Salvation Army people were. They were very earnest about
saving mankind rather than punishing it."

As worthy as those ideals were, neither son maintained his Army
faith. At twelve Bill was working for twenty-five cents an hour as a janitor
in a factory, a job his father had found him and one he resented because
his buddies would be frolicking at the lake while he toiled. He was also
playing trumpet on the streets with the local Army band and attending
church: "I had what I consider a spiritual or religious experience many

times. Every Sunday morning it was a call to the altar to be forgiven of your sins with a sermon well preached about good and evil and black and white. But around age fifteen I vividly recall telling my dad that I no longer wanted to go to church or Sunday school. I played in the band, giving a church service right on the street corner, but I had reached a point where it wasn't cool. Dad was a wonderful guy and when I said I didn't really feel like going anymore, he said, 'Okay, Bill, you don't have to go'. But I still went for a while."

Herb too would leave the Army church: "I was a boy soprano at the time and my father, being the man that he was, was forever seeking opportunities for his kids. He was very active in the Kiwanis Club and through that met one of the top voice teachers in Denver. She was Episcopalian and recruited me to sing with the boys' choir at St. John's Cathedral in Denver. I really liked the liturgy, and the majesty of the service just captured me and so I have been an Episcopalian ever since then."

With Pearl Harbor and America's entry into the global war, the unemployed of the Depression were being called up for service or working in the military-supply and munitions fields ("The Men's Social Centers, so recently swamped with applicants, gradually became almost deserted," *Marching to Glory* notes). The Ellison brothers, nearing their fifties and engaged in good works, continued serving with the religious Army in the U.S.

Ben and his family moved yet again, this time to Seattle in 1943, as the city was emerging as a major player in the defense industry. The Puget Sound area became a key naval base and tens of thousands of troops trained at nearby Fort Lewis. The Boeing Company evolved into the primary manufacturer of heavy bombers flown by the U.S. Army Air Force. Herb and Bill attended three different high schools in the area as the Ellisons shifted from one house to another. While Bill played a little football in high school, he was too small to make the team, but he boxed and did a lot of swimming and competitive diving.

Then in 1947 Ben was called on to run the men's social service store in Los Angeles, one of the Army's largest, fed by dozens of collection trucks. None of the kids wanted to leave the Pacific Northwest. "Bill saved my life at that point, as he often did," Herb reminisces. "I was just beginning the second half of my senior year of high school and the idea of leaving Seattle and transitioning down to California to some strange new place and to a new high school was more than I could bear. I really was anxious about it."

Bill was a freshman at the University of Washington and a member of Chi Psi (the first fraternity founded in the U.S. on stated principles of brotherhood). The brothers schemed to stay in Seattle while their folks took their reluctant younger sister, Beverly, to L.A. "Bill and I had been through a lot together, first with a move to Seattle which uprooted us from an environment that we loved," Herb says. "But he was a good buddy to have during these transition years. He's the irrepressible fixer and said he would talk to the fraternity and see if we could both live there.

"I recently was talking to one of the members of the fraternity, Bill Gates Senior, and he said, 'Well, how did you even get that worked out? It was against fraternity council rules to have non-fraternity members living in the house.'

"I said, 'I don't know, but Bill did it.' So I finished the second half of my senior year there. Fraternities in those days had a very high proportion of veterans. It was very disciplined and we wore coats and ties to dinner every night." Later, when Beverly became a college freshman, she rejoined her brothers by attending the U of W too.

ENTERING CIVVIE STREET

Meanwhile, in Los Angeles, Ben Ellison had reached a crossroads in his career, as had the Salvation Army. The organization had changed its focus during the war and adopted a new philosophy, summarized in *Marching to Glory*: "Above all, the Army had to abandon the idea that the social institutions were a 'business,' to employ men merely to raise revenue for the work; the purpose of the Men's Social Service Department to make 'better men' must be reaffirmed."

Ben made a decision that would have a profound impact on the entire Ellison clan. In 1949 – increasingly frustrated by the Salvation Army's shift in emphasis and its on-going bureaucracy – he felt that he'd paid his dues and it was time now to strike out on his own as a private entrepreneur. After operating the biggest moneymaker of all the Army's

The young Ellison family poses for a formal portrait in civilian dress: Ben and Esther flank their two sons, Herb and Bill, and their daughter Beverly.

retail outlets in the U.S., with greatly expanded electrical and furniture-repairing shops, he saw a niche to open his own thrift-store business on a for-profit basis. Orlo recognized the same opportunity and left the Army to join Ben in this private venture. Son Bill's memory, from more than half a century ago, is that his father and uncle opened a store together in Denver. But the partnership was short-lived, he explains: "Both were pretty strong-willed guys – a recurring trait with Ellisons – and they went their separate ways."

Ben and Esther moved to Sacramento, California's state capital, which had just become a city as its population burgeoned amid Cold War fears that drove local military-industrial manufacturing. During the 1950s the state government also ballooned to become a major employer. Ben arranged with war veterans' organizations there to collect clothes and other goods, which he would sell in a more customer-friendly style.

Orlo, meanwhile, opened a thrift store in 1951 outside Los Angeles (Pasadena, Bill believes) and also linked it with veterans. As Army Major George Duplain told a *Los Angeles Times* reporter decades later, "Orlo did his best to talk me into not becoming a Salvation Army officer. 'George, there's millions to be made with the public's concern for veterans now that the war is over,' Orlo would tell me."

The Ellisons had taught their younger brother Robert the trade so well that he also opened a private store, to be followed by Walter and the youngest, John. "Today," says Savers' chairman, Tom Ellison, "there are a lot of extended Ellisons in the thrift-store business, including my aunt Beverly and her husband in Tampa, Florida. He worked for my dad from the early '60s to the very early '70s before he moved east and started his own business." Obviously, Ben's decision to become an entrepreneur was the beginning of an Ellison assault on the American thrift industry that would expand to embrace succeeding generations.

Tom now looks back on his ancestors' life-transforming acts more than half a century ago and reflects: "The brothers left the Salvation Army in a controversy because they wanted to be entrepreneurs. They'd asked if they could have a performance clause in their contracts because the Army paid almost subsistence wages and they would be transferred all around the country, either opening new or fixing old thrift stores and making the Army a lot of money. Now it was post-war and it was inevitable that they would want to own their own businesses. But it didn't make sense for the Army to do that." (To this day, Tom continues to respect the organization: "I personally donate to the Salvation Army, I believe in their mission that much. If you walk in indigent and need a meal or a jacket from one of their stores, you'll get it.")

The early operators were pioneering new territory. The Sally Ann had been honing techniques to gather goods, including telephone solicitation and mail-back cards, but this had been an entirely internal operation. Now Ben and Orlo Ellison were working in collaboration with a charity, which would pick up merchandise in its own name and be paid a set fee to deliver to an independently run store. While the brothers did begin with vets' groups – popular with the public in those years right after the World War II – the net was soon cast wider. A daughter of Walter Ellison had Down's syndrome, and so he worked with charities serving children with various disabilities. Not surprisingly, the family's first profit-making stores were not beauty queens. "By comparison today, they would be classified as junk stores, nothing like the stores that we build today," Bill points out.

Back in Seattle, while Herb was studying European and American history and the French and German languages, his brother took a degree at the U of W's business school. Like his dad, Bill had dreamed of running his own show: "The major corporations came to campus to recruit the new graduates, and right then I decided that I didn't want to work for any big companies. I had a burning desire to be in business for myself."

It would take a few distracting years to harness his dream. At college the good-looking young man met Sue Norquist, an auburn-haired student of Scandinavian heritage who went on to work in an administrative office on campus. They were married in June 1950. After graduation Bill tried several jobs in Seattle, including printing sales, none of which he enjoyed. "I had a liking for radio, and television was on its way then, and I thought I would get into that business. And KIRO was the number-one radio station in Seattle." Before he could land a job there, the Korean War interceded in 1950 to send him spinning off in a new direction. At college he had joined the Reserve Officer Training Corps, the ROTC, and received a commission as a second lieutenant. When the war between North and South Korea hotted up, western nations leapt in to battle the Communist North and its mainland-Chinese allies. Among the Americans called up was the twenty-two-year-old Bill Ellison.

He began active duty at Fort Lawton, a historic army reserve post in northwest Seattle. "My commanding officer was a West Point colonel who took a liking to me; we played golf together and my wife and I were entertained at their place for dinner. He became like a godfather to me." Because Bill had set up a training center for military units at the base and was receiving letters of commendation for his work, the CO removed his name from the list of ROTC officers heading to Korea. Eventually Bill ran the officers' club: "It was the hardest work I had ever done in the army because there was an average of anywhere from 600 to 1,000 personnel who were either on their way to Korea or coming back and would spend their transition at Fort Lawton. Either way, they were celebrating, so it was a crazy place – we had military police all over. It was good experience." Even when his CO left for Korea himself, Bill managed to serve his two years in Seattle.

A civilian again, he recalled his father's admonition to keep doggedly pursuing anything you really want in life. Bill wanted to work for

KIRO. The first station west of the Mississippi to operate at 50,000 watts, it had a relaxed announcing style that prompted the nickname "The Friendly Station." He remembers, "I went to their Queen Anne Avenue office three or four times a week to see the sales manager and one day I said, 'I'm just going to keep coming, so hire me to get rid of me.' So he hired me on the spot and I began going door to door trying to sell radio time to merchants in downtown Seattle. I think my salary was about $200 a month. Over the next year I had doors closed in my face many times, but I kept going and started to create a little bit of business after a while."

By then he and Sue had started a family. Debra was born in 1952 and Jeff two years later – just about the time Bill got a fateful phone call from his dad, still operating his lone store in California:

"Bill, how would you like to be your own boss? And make some money at the same time? I'll help you if you're interested in coming to San Francisco and we'll open a store together." Ben would put up half the startup capital.

"And," as Bill recollected more than fifty years later, "that's how it began."

"We were afraid the crowded mezzanine would collapse."

FAMILY ENTERPRISE

CHAPTER THREE

It was 1954, a time when only 154 Americans had incomes of more than $1 million. That year, RCA introduced the first color TV set on the market. Movie theaters were featuring *The Caine Mutiny* and *The Day the Earth Stood Still*. In Memphis a nineteen-year-old named Elvis Presley cut his first commercial recording at Sun Records. In Detroit the $30-million Northland was launched as the world's largest shopping center with the largest department store built in America since the Crash of '29. And in San Francisco, on Saturday, December 11, William O. Ellison was finally in business for himself, opening the little Purple Heart Thrift Store in the yeasty Mission District. Total revenue for the day: $448.

The first privately operated thrift shop in the city was housed in an old theater at Mission and 29th, fronting on the sidewalk in a commercial area where long-established middle-class Irish and Italian residents had yielded to immigrants after World War II. Waves of Central and South Americans seeking economic opportunity and political haven turned one of San Francisco's oldest neighborhoods into a kind of barrio – a melting pot of Hispanic cultures, from Bolivian, Nicaraguan, and Guatemalan to Mexican and even Cuban.

Into this colorful working-class quarter of burrito joints, Salvadoran bakeries, and beauty shops called *salon de bellezas* came a young business-man of Scots-Irish descent. He had $8,500 borrowed from his father and the words of his former boss at KIRO Radio resounding in his ears: "If you can run one of those stores well, you can run ten."

Opposite: Bill (right) with actor Darren McGavin and Miss Tacoma in 1967.

Bill's first business venture, the Purple Heart Thrift Store, opened December 1954 in San Francisco's Mission District, with first-day sales of $448.

That initial store was all of thirty feet wide and seventy deep, its basement bursting with the merchandise collected in the name of the Woodrow Wilson Chapter #15 of the Military Order of the Purple Heart, a charitable organization that supported American veterans wounded in action. "This was a store that we would use as a storage room now," Bill says all these years later. "By comparison to today, it was a real junk store, but it was successful."

Sue Ellison moved with her daughter and son to the Bay Area under protest, unhappy about leaving her hometown, Seattle. Like most mothers in the 1950s – who grew up during wartime when their own mothers often had to go out to work – she was content to stay home and raise her children. Four months earlier, her husband had arrived in San Francisco ahead of her to labor with his dad and some of Ben's employees, down from Sacramento, to transform the decrepit theater into a workable retail space. They made all the racks themselves and, for easier customer access, hung some of the clothes on hangers rather than burying them in bins. On the day of the grand opening, the temperature was so torrid that racks and other fixtures sank into the store's asphalt floor and couldn't be shifted. Even so, Bill was thrilled with the first day's sales, meager as they sound today.

Women's hats, shoes, and purses then all cost a quarter. "Every week we'd send out a hundred men's white dress shirts for laundering and would sell ninety of them because they were clean." Among the unusual items he managed to peddle were boxes with a World War I airplane propeller, fuselage, and all the wheels. "I just wanted to move it all out. Later I learned that you don't have to give things away. In those early days I was an easy mark for some of our customers because I was the boss and they befriended me – and I was just a proper twenty-six-year-old."

He instinctively realized the power of what Sam Walton, the founder of Wal-Mart, calls the ten-foot rule: Whenever you come within ten feet of a customer, look them in the eye and ask if you can help them. As Bill explains, "It is just a human encounter between one person and another. How do you feel when you walk into a store and wander around and nobody ever speaks to you? You walk out again. It's like somebody walking into your house and you go the other way and don't talk to them. It is human love: caring for other people and indicating that you do."

In those early days he paid himself out of the till in his role as a combination store manager, sorter, and pricer. At most he had eight employees: "I was hands-on eight days a week, twelve hours a day. We had a guy who repaired refrigerators, which were not all that common then – a lot of people still had ice boxes. But he did refrigerators and washing machines. . . . I had a couple of cashiers in that first store for many years. I think they were in their forties and they sort of adopted me not only as a boss but as a son of their own. They acted like they were the mother of the store; if something dishonest was going on, they would report it to me."

There were enough honest and eager low-income shoppers to make the store a success. In 1955 Bill was emboldened enough to approach a bank for a $12,000 loan to open his second location in the city of San Jose, a food-processing and manufacturing center southeast of San Francisco Bay. Asked about his business plan, the cocky young entrepreneur replied, "I think one day we'll have a hundred stores." ("Grandiosity," he says today with a smile.) That was the last store he would own for a long while.

"There was some unrest in southern California about some of the stores operated by other people as private enterprises. Actually, that problem was created by Goodwill Industries, who did it because we were such strong competition for them; there was no competition in the state until we came along. California passed a law that said any solicitation for goods had to be done exclusively by the charity and any collections had to be done under the ownership of the charity. Somehow or another we legally turned it around and managed to keep operating."

He turned it around by restructuring his legal agreements with the non-profits. "This was called a buy/sell contract. They would solicit the merchandise and we would buy it from them. Very little difference."

Yet there was one major difference: while Bill would finance the launch of any new stores, essentially he was now merely operating rather than owning them. In 1960 he incorporated a company called the Salvage Management Corporation. He had all the headaches involved in overseeing the charities' pickup programs and the staff and stock of the retail outlets – for a fifty-fifty split of the profits. "But then after a store was organized, we discovered that the charity would just discharge us after it was doing well. They'd say, 'Well, we don't need you anymore, you've done your work – so goodbye'." In one year alone, he lost half a dozen stores that way and many, if not most of them, eventually folded.

There were other problems, including employees who learned the business from Bill and then went out on their own. Among them was his sister Beverly's husband, Rod Tullis, who opened competing stores and did well with them. ("Of all the people who left," Tom remembers, "he purposely set out to be as far away from our business as possible – in Florida.") At Bill's second store in Redwood City, the first to be called Thrift Village, he had an employee named Albert. "He was a personal friend – a charming guy and a professional violinist from France by trade. But Albert was having the pickup truck stop at a store he'd opened quietly and they were dropping the goods there before they got to my store. The goods started to get less and less. One day a truck driver who was bothered by the procedure asked me if I knew Albert had this store in Redwood City, a little hole-in-the-wall around the corner from our big store there."

Years later, Bill would say, "Our past was littered with unwise decisions." What upset him most of all was that decision by some charities to elbow him out of the outlets he'd financed and got up and running for them: "After you get knocked down a few times like that, it sort of gets your attention. There had to be another way to do this."

The other way was to once again own his stores outright. In 1966 he turned his attention north – to the state he'd left for California – and opened a company-controlled outlet in Renton, Washington. Just southeast of Seattle, the freshwater port on Lake Washington was a growing industrial city of 18,000 with a steel foundry and the Boeing Company's plant, which had been building aircraft there since World War II. The 8,900-square-foot store was in its own stand-alone building, which in bold letters on the front and sides heralded itself with a name then in common use by other thrift stores operating in California: Value Village.

The following year, in an old J.C. Penney store in Tacoma, Washington, another Village was launched with a splashy debut. It featured the actor Darren McGavin, who'd starred on TV as Mickey Spillane's tough-guy detective, Mike Hammer, and in film as a drug pusher in the Frank Sinatra starring vehicle *The Man with the Golden Arm*. Growing up, McGavin had once lived at the Dyslin Boys Ranch in Tacoma, a group home and vocational training center for disadvantaged kids, and was eager to support the charity with fund-raising events. After Bill first approached him through a mutual friend to appear at the opening of the Redwood City store, the two of them had become pals. The actor even invited the Ellison kids to tour a Hollywood studio. For the Tacoma launch, he brought a wardrobe of clothing owned by celebrities such as movie star Robert Stack and singer Rosemary Clooney, which was auctioned off to help finance the boys' ranch. And of course the presence of McGavin and a pretty Miss Tacoma helped publicize the new store. "The mezzanine got so crowded at the grand opening that people were afraid it was going to collapse," Tom recalls.

A happy Bill Ellison relaxes at a retreat with his sons, Tom (left) and Jeff, who had begun learning the business the hard way – from the ground floor up.

CALIFORNIA DREAMIN' — AND A DARK CLOUD

Although Sue was excited about the possibility of returning to the Pacific Northwest, that move wouldn't happen for a few years. Their third and last child had been born in 1956: Thomas, a brother for Debra and Jeff. They were fair-haired California kids at a time when the state was blossoming as an almost-instant new society of non-conformity and fresh ideas, and when San Francisco itself was a hotbed where first the beat generation and then the '60s protesters and hippies flourished.

The Ellison offspring were far from social rebels, however, growing up amid the suburban sprawl sixteen miles south of their father's first store. They and their flock of dogs lived in the serene little city of Mill-brae (mid-'60s population: 15,000), in a nice house with a big backyard and a large swimming pool in a middle-class area high on a hill above the San Francisco international airport. "In the early days, our dad was a guy who spent everything he ever made," Tom recalls. "He wanted the family to have a good experience, so if it meant spending money to build a pool in the backyard, he would do it for us. He didn't worry about saving for a rainy day, and in a way I kind of admire that because it worked out for him. It wasn't like we lived an extravagant lifestyle, but we enjoyed life. We took a vacation or two a year, which a lot of people didn't do in those days."

All three offspring were bright young things. "Like all big sisters," Tom says of Debbie, "she was a part-time ally and a part-time enemy. But she had a lot of hot girlfriends, so I enjoyed the parade of California girls that came to our backyard pool. She was the one girl, so she was the princess. My father was very protective of her – we were all his pride and joy but on her sixteenth birthday, she got a brand-new car and on mine he showed me how to buy a used car." As adults, brother and sister would continue to have a loving relationship.

In 1980 Jeff's high school buddy Scott Blomquist became the company's new one-man advertising and marketing department for all of North America.

Jeff was a good student. Scott Blomquist, a high-school friend, drove the stores' pickup trucks with him on weekends and went on to work with him in the family business. "Jeff was really smart and did well in school. He played guitar and other instruments and had an interest in zoology and bird-watching. He didn't play a lot of organized sports, but he was athletic in swimming. And he had a job making stained glass after high school." In Bill Ellison's words, "Jeff is a little more mellow in some ways – not quite as explosive as Tom is and he smells the flowers along the way."

Tom, not yet into his teens, was another whiz at school, but Bill says, "Teachers had a hard time controlling him in class because everything was too easy for him and he'd get bored." Tom remembers that "as a kid I spent a lot of time in those dusty old junk stores – which is really what they were then, small and not that far from home. I used to like to play in the stores and in my twelfth summer I first started to work on a regular basis in the store. Doing anything they told me – cleaning up, and sometimes they'd let me run the cash register with an adult standing next to me."

One of his major aspirations outside of school was to own a big car someday, like the fancy ones his dad drove. Father gave son his first driving lessons at twelve on a quiet street in Millbrae. "He had a brand-new black 1968 Eldorado and I loved it. He probably bribed me to wash the car with him so that I could go for a lesson. I was washing and he was talking about the company and said that someday he was going to have a hundred stores – and when that happened I would probably be his vice-president of international marketing or something. And that stuck with me."

As idyllic as family life seemed, there was a black cloud looming over the Ellisons. Bill was grappling with a personal challenge: he seemed to have a hereditary disposition to alcoholism, like his father and mother. Scott, Jeff's friend, noticed Bill's problem with liquor when the boys were in high school: "Jeff and I would sometimes do some knucklehead things and Bill would get angry – and I could tell he was under the influence. His wife was cordial and quiet and behind the scenes. Individually, both were wonderful people and Sue was a pretty good anchor for him with her high moral standards and religion."

But by 1968 the drinking had become so bad that an attorney friend who'd been to Sunday dinner with the Ellisons told his host: "You know what, Bill? You don't drink so good. Look at yourself." Bill decided to attend an Alcoholics Anonymous meeting in the Bay area's San Mateo County. The people he met that evening offered him loving care, he recalls – "they embraced me." Over the long run, this dramatic move – publicly confessing that he'd succumbed to the family failing – would help save him and his business.

Not long after joining AA, he convinced his seventy-three-year-old father to acompany him to a couple of sessions, but not until about the third meeting did Ben publicly acknowledge his own problem. His decision was a poignant one, his grandson Tom remembers: "My dad took him to the AA meeting and he stood up for the first time and said, 'Hi, I am Ben and I am an alcoholic.' And that was the first time that he had admitted it." After recounting a brief but moving summary of his life to fellow AAs, Ben told Bill he'd join him again the next night. But, suffering from a heart condition and physically depleted, he had a bad coughing spell overnight and then suddenly fell silent and died, on June 3, 1968. (His wife, Esther, died, aged seventy-four, at the home of her daughter, Beverly, in Tampa, Florida.)

Ben's death stiffened his son's resolve to stay sober and keep attending AA meetings. For the next few years he got caught up in the organization's positive philosophy, sponsored other alcoholics pursuing the famous twelve-step program, and helped spread its message through inspiring motivational talks at junior high schools ("That was the most rewarding time of my life, talking to kids who had problems in their families").

Tom was only twelve when his grandfather died. "He was extremely special to me. He had a really great sense of humor and I never saw him in a bad light because of his drinking."

At the time, both Tom and Jeff were preoccupied by the usual things that intrigued boys of their age. And they had a role model in John Bacon, a tall young man courting their sister, who worked in a gas station and drove hot-looking cars. The middle son in a family of five kids – and painfully shy around strangers – he had a father in the retail business too, as chief security officer for I. Magnin, a major western department-store chain. John lived in Burlingame, neighboring Millbrae, and attended the same high school as Debbie but didn't meet her until the summer of his graduation year. He went to the Ellisons' for an end-of-term pool party. She was sixteen, a sophomore, and he was two years older and on his way to college.

"We were kind of friends for a couple of months until we started going out," he says, "and I kept coming back and they invited me to dinner and then I was there every night." (As Bill says, "John never left. He spent the summer with us and we fed him and made him grow big and tall.")

"Debbie's mom was pretty strict, protective. If we went out on the weekend, we had a curfew and during school nights she would boot me out at nine. It was a very innocent time. They seemed to be a pretty close family back then. They did Sunday dinners and I'd be invited and if they went out to dinner, I'd be invited, and even went on short trips with them. During that summer, as I was just getting to know Bill, I had a couple of other jobs and was making pretty good money. But he asked me if I was interested in coming to work for him."

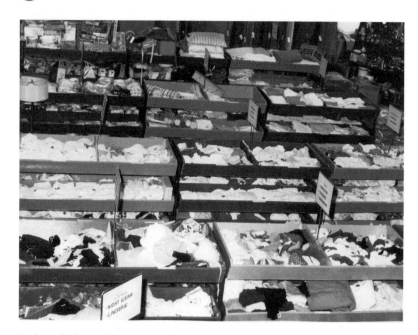

In the early days, John Bacon recalls, only some clothes were hung neatly. "Everything else would be in bins or boxes — massive rows of giant bins."

Although John knew nothing about the thrift-store business, he agreed to work part-time as he attended junior college. That was the beginning of a relationship with the Ellisons and Bill's company that would endure for three decades. He started in January 1969 as a furniture and shoe pricer making $1.60 an hour, much less than he did at the service station as an assistant manager. Shortly after, he pitched in as Bill opened a third outlet in San Jose, a city of little more than 100,000 southeast of the Bay.

He describes the Redwood City store as funky, an odd-shaped building where none of the angles were square. Nor were the staff: they were an intriguing medley of young and old, mostly blacks and Hispanics, working for the pipe-smoking, slow-talking Rod Tullis. An organization for the mentally handicapped supplied the merchandise. "Back then supply was not really the issue; we had plenty of goods," John says. "All that they hung at the time was ladies' clothing and a few items of men's clothing. Everything else would be thrown in bins or boxes, massive rows of giant bins – kind of what you would think of an old thrift store years ago. Things were color-coordinated, as opposed to sized, and none of the children's clothing was hung."

He cleaned the shoes, clipped pairs together with so-called hog rings that sometimes ruined the shoes, and then put them out willy-nilly, never displayed by size. Furniture pricing was based on simple supply and demand: "If you were down on mattresses, the mattress price went up."

Within a few months, he was doing weekends at the Purple Heart store in San Francisco, being managed by Sue's cousin Bud Norquist who (along with his brother-in-law, Steve Moore) worked with Bill – before going out on his own with a western thrift-store chain, which his son eventually took over. "Again," John says about that original store, "there was a really great group of characters. A cashier who had been there for years and was kind of like the matriarch and ran things. She followed me everywhere; I don't know if she spied on me for Bill or if she just didn't trust me. She checked on everybody." Coming from his homogenous white community, he was fascinated by the way Asian, Samoan, and Afro-American employees ran their own departments in a protective way, often playing jokes on one another. "I did furniture deliveries because you got a delivery fee, and let me tell you, delivering in San Francisco was a real treat. You're going up four or five stories with mattresses into places that were amazing."

John – artistic and highly visual – was also studying architecture at junior college but found the academic work difficult. He had what would be diagnosed as attention deficit disorder, ADD. After about eighteen months, as he kept switching courses, a counsellor asked him what he really wanted to do.

It was decided for him. In 1970, Bill agreed to move the family back to Washington, where they settled in the residential city of Bellevue, just east of Seattle across Lake Washington. He had the store in Renton and was opening more company-owned Value Villages in the King County communities of Burien and Lake City, south and north of Seattle.

John and Debbie had become serious about one another and she didn't want to leave him behind. Bill invited her boyfriend to come work for him up north for a lean $300 a month. John would soon be managing the Burien store – but not before putting in his apprenticeship at the Lake

City outlet by driving a truck and picking up goods in a charity's name along with other drivers employed by Bill.

WASHINGTON WORKIN' — AND A GOOD PARTNER

Meanwhile, the Renton store was working with a new non-profit called the Northwest Center, which since 1965 had been assisting mentally handicapped children, originally with funding from the Boeing Employees' Good Neighbor Fund. Jim McClurg, who later became executive director of the Center, says that "when Bill Ellison first wrote a letter to the board, members of the finance committee were a bit suspicious – what he was offering sounded too good to be true. He wanted to solicit used clothing in our name and give us a percentage of the profit from the stores: 'We'll just send you a check every month.'

"In the mid-'60s, nobody was doing this sort of thing. But this group of volunteers weren't stupid. They invited Bill to make a presentation to the full board, who said they liked the way it sounded." For the right to use the Center's name, he would contact donors, pick up used goods, sell them in the store, and split the profits fifty-fifty. "We had no capital outlay, we weren't being asked to put anything on the table – except something else that's important: our reputation. It was probably one of the two most important things our board ever decided."

The arrangement would continue uninterrupted until near the decade's end when, according to Jim – then at the Center teaching children and young adults with severe disability challenges – "the attorney-general of the state got to be very unhappy with us. He started to get concerned that this was an illegitimate operation, that the Northwest Center was just a front for a private vendor making money in the name of a non-profit. Katie Dolan and John Chapman and others at the Center went to fight the battle. The state said that to be legitimate, the people doing the phone-calling and the pickup of goods had to be employees of the Center. That got us out of immediate trouble with the attorney-general. We remained on a profit-share basis and though we paid for the drivers and solicitors, Bill's company reimbursed the Northwest Center for our costs."

John Bacon went from managing a Village in Burien, Washington, to opening one in Seattle – and eventually became executive vice-president.

For the next few years, the Center's collection staff worked out of the Renton location. In 1970, when the Ellisons moved to Washington, Bill changed the name of his Salvage Management Corporation to Thrift Village Inc. and a year later officially moved its legal headquarters from California to Renton – the same year it expanded into its third state, Oregon, with a store in Portland.

At first the corporate base of operations was in the Renton store itself. Among the early employees was Marie Gunn, a widow from North

Controller Bill Fraser came aboard as a suit-and-tie Price Waterhouse accountant and at first had to work out of a cubbyhole under a stairwell.

Dakota, who became Bill's devoted secretary ("I think she felt almost like a godmother to me") and worked for him for long years before trying unsuccessfully to run her own thrift-store business in Arizona. Bill hired a general manager named George Seferos, a friend from Alcoholics Anonymous who'd been an aggressive real-estate sales manager with no retail experience. He later recruited a senior Price Waterhouse accountant, Bill Fraser, who comments on George's hiring: "That's what Bill did – he hired friends and and told them to take it and run with it."

The twenty-seven-year-old newcomer hadn't known his new boss or anything about his business before joining the company as controller in 1973. Bill Ellison – no longer managing any stores for charities – had plans to expand beyond his eight company-owned operations. But he needed tighter reins on his finances if he wanted to land a federal Small Business Administration loan. Bill Fraser, just five years out of university, saw the business then as a proper mess: "I didn't research it very thoroughly or I might not have joined it. Bill and George oversaw the stores and there were no district managers. It was pretty loose. They had a book-keeper who pumped all the accounting into a service bureau in Renton. It was a couple of years since they'd had decent accounting practices back in California. My first day, when I showed up in my Price Waterhouse suit, they took me to meet the Renton store manager and I felt a bit out of place." His first office was in a cubbyhole under the stairwell.

Not long after, the headquarters moved to a former stationery store in a concrete-block building on Park Avenue across the street from the store. Bill Fraser and George had windowless offices, Bill Ellison larger but unfancy quarters. Half the 3,000 square feet was devoted to phone solicitors for the Northwest Center, which housed its old trucks in a rent-ed warehouse up the road.

John Bacon had married Debbie in 1972 and after managing the Burien location had his first chance to open a Value Village two years later on Rainier Avenue in south Seattle. "When I first took over as manager in Burien, we were still doing everything the same way and I was really intrigued by retail. I spent a lot of time in other retail stores in the malls and that led to my first attempt at trying to departmentalize. I started sizing clothing instead of just color-coordinating it. At the time, it was basic small/medium/large and we would do pant sizes, but you'd have to go through a rack of thirty feet and look at every pair of pants for a size thirty-two. There was no budget for anything, so I used old shower-cur-tain hooks and manila tags as the first rings to separate sizes." He also rearranged clothing racks to create distinctive departments of ladies' and men's clothing. Eventually his stores were the first Villages to hang chil-dren's clothing on racks, rather than leaving them jumbled in bins. "Most of the other managers who had been around a long time looked at me as if I was crazy. I was trying to make it simpler – when the philosophy back then was to make it as easy as you can for the employee instead of for the customer."

Then in Seattle's Rainier store John introduced a color palette that became standard in other locations for many years: yellow, brown, and orange. "It was without a doubt the most beautiful store that we had. We got some press from it and some people from the Goodwill stores would come in and we'd catch them looking at it. This was a new generation of the Value Village stores. I had a lot of passion on the design side, but there was a ton of people who worked so hard in putting this together." On opening day, parking was so tight that a woman's car smashed into the store's large plate-glass front window, and a furniture clerk had to spend the night on watch until the glass could be replaced the next morning.

By now another member of the extended family had left junior college in California to get into the business. John's brother, Mike, had worked a couple of summers as a laborer for John; as a full-time employee he became assistant manager of three stores over eighteen months, starting at his brother's Rainier Street location. "I knew in the first year this was for me," Mike says now. "Family's important to me and I felt comfortable with anything with a family orientation."

THE NEXT GENERATION

In 1974, about a decade after their grandfather Ben and uncle Orlo had died, the third generation of Ellisons also entered the thrift-store trade. Acting on their father's suggestion and encouraged by their brother-in-law John's example, Jeff and Tom both joined the company. Jeff, who'd married his high-school sweetheart, Sandy, was learning the store-management side as a trainee. His younger brother started on the ground floor in an embryonic enterprise their dad was developing to go beyond the selling of used goods.

During his first year in high school, Tom had worked for the Northwest Center as a helper on a collection truck. Then he was a part-time salesman in men's-wear shops during the rest of his school years. In one of the stores he met and started dating a girl named Sue Casey, who was working there too. A couple of months after graduating, he went into the family trade. "I had high hopes to make really good money and I was let down the day they told me that I'd get a salary of $500 a month – there was no negotiation – and I think it worked out to be about $3 a hour." Tom arrived at a time when the business was venturing into new waters: "In those days my father's stated goal was to get the company up to fifty-per-cent new-merchandise sales in the stores."

As Bill Fraser explains, "It was an ego thing for Bill. There was a separate new-merchandise profit center called ENS Sales [for the initials of its three partners, including another retailer]. They'd buy liquidation and close-out merchandise for pennies on the dollar. Bob Reilly was running it; he was Sue Ellison's cousin and had worked in a men's clothing store. And Bob had a pickup truck."

"That was my first job here," Tom says. "Delivering, and being the stock boy in the warehouse in Seattle. So I delivered this merchandise to our stores in Seattle and one in Portland, Oregon – and I never really liked that angle of the business. We sold Anchor Hocking glassware, for example, and new pots and pans and some new clothing. My father believed that someday the used-merchandise flow could be interrupted or stop. And there were all kinds of surplus stores that grew into discount chains [selling new merchandise] back in the '60s and the '70s. But all I knew was the margins were bad and we couldn't compete with the big mass merchants. Had we been doing it even twenty years later, we would have been out of business because you can't compete with Target and Wal-Mart."

A year later Tom was pricing furniture six days and almost every night each week and opening and closing the Renton store on weekends. Some days, however, he played hooky to take flying lessons. His dad had taken him and Jeff to the Renton airport for a flight on a Cessna to see if they wanted to be recreational pilots. Later, Bill decided he didn't want to learn to fly, but his sons were hooked. "We did it during work because we could get away with it and our dad encouraged us," says Tom, who much later bought his own float plane (which he has since sold).

Although his boss was his older brother, who by then was the store's manager, they got on well together. "There was never a time that the store was open when there was not an Ellison in the room," he says. Then at a ripe young nineteen, he too became a manager – of the Lake

Fred Pesterkoff, a Lake City, Washington, employee for three decades, celebrates his retirement before visiting the Graceland estate of his idol, Elvis.

City store, where John Bacon had served his apprenticeship, in a vibrant inner-city neighborhood.

"It was a tiny 6,500 square feet and hadn't made any money in two or three years at least. My father's general manager, George Seferos, had said, 'You know, there are problem people there. The store hasn't been well managed.' He warned me and so I went in and observed for a little bit and realized that I did need to start making some changes. I saw staff who were focused on anything but their jobs and the biggest problem was the second person in charge, the production supervisor. At the end of the first week, I found myself sitting in my office with the door closed, letting her go. She was probably in her early thirties and I was nineteen and dripping-wet behind the ears. But it was necessary. Today I would have done it the day that I got there, knowing what I know now, but then I could feel myself turning tomato-red, feeling bad about it, guilty, all the things that you feel. She had kids and that was one of the problems: one of her daughters worked in the store and got away with murder."

In the year Tom was there, the store became profitable. "I replaced an awful lot of the staff right away and then hired a person who became a very key employee for us, Sue Fish. I hired her as a cashier and she ultimately became a district manager who helped us open up a lot of stores. She was a year or two older than me and may have done a couple of years of community college, but Sue is classic in that she started with us at the very bottom of the ladder and worked her way right up. She is very outgoing, a quick learner, a deeply caring, dependable person." (A few years later, when he'd approach her to be a store manager, she broke down and cried.)

Fred Pesterkoff, whom Bill Ellison had hired, was another employee at Lake City who seemed like a member of the family. Because he had problems handling money, often giving it away to others, Tom helped him save and arranged to buy a car for him. "That started a tradition at the Lake City store that every manager who followed was the manager of Fred's bank account. Fred's paycheck would come in and he would get a little allowance and the balance would go into a savings account. My dad has always been pretty much people-first – and surprise! it pays off too." (Three decades later, Fred was still working at the Lake City store and, as a great Elvis fan, was rewarded with an all-expense-paid trip to Graceland. He died six weeks after his retirement party – just a couple of years short of the thirty-five years he'd wanted to spend with the company.)

The business was such a seat-of-the-pants operation that everybody just pitched in to make things happen. Tom tells the story of the time in 1975 when the small Burien store John was running moved up the road: "In those days we wouldn't have even thought about going out of business to move a store, so as soon as the store closed at nine P.M., we started to move stuff over. We hired Northwest Center truck drivers and they let us borrow the trucks and we moved until about three A.M. – and then slept for three or four hours to open up the next day in the new location."

The Ellison boys had come into the company at a time when an energy-sparked economic recession was gripping the globe and Wall Street's bellwether Dow Jones Industrial Average was bottoming out. Thrift Village Inc.'s finances reflected the faltering American economy. After landing the Small Business Administration loan of about $200,000 in 1974, the company expanded to Lynnwood, Rainier Valley, and Spokane, Washington. "And that's when we started getting into trouble," Bill Fraser reflects. "With the recession, sales were down and George Seferos and I put together a staged plan – different degrees of drasticness. Spokane was a huge store, a former skating rink. We'd bought the property and then we decided to lease out half for a Social Security office."

"We didn't have any money," Tom recalls, "and so when it came to store expansion or setting up a new relationship with a not-for-profit partner – or just getting money from the bank to make ends meet – it was tough. We couldn't get arrested in those days. We couldn't borrow money from anybody."

"The company had one luxury item, a five-year-old motor home. One day in January 1975 my dad and I took a day off together to go skiing in that motor home. But we didn't have enough cash in the bank to make payroll and we were just getting by. And we were talking about ways to make cash – and one of those was to sell the motor home. It was that tight." In fact, they didn't even have enough equity in the vehicle to make it worthwhile selling.

The financial challenges contributed to a deteriorating situation at home. But there was another problem: During the early '70s, starting to consider himself cured, Bill had resumed drinking, a bit at a time, until the disease consumed him again. Bill Fraser remembers those days: "At lunch we'd have a couple of drinks and, when trying to make a deal with a banker in California, we'd have a three-martini lunch. It wasn't getting-drunk kind of drinking – it was more maintenance drinking, I suppose." Another executive who joined the company later says, "Bill would tell you he drank all the profits back then."

In desperation, Sue Ellison had joined Al-Anon, which serves the families and friends of alcoholics. Hoping that if her husband hit rock bottom, he'd wake up to his alcoholism, she ordered him out of the house. In 1975, with their marriage fallen apart, he and Sue were

Tom (back row, in sunglasses) and former football star Hugh McElhenny (far right) witness the launch of a Thrift Village in San Jose, California.

divorced. The shock of that action did have one positive effect: it helped him go on the wagon once and for all ("I had to take a few hard punches, but I came back with no doubt in my mind").

Looking back on those days, Tom says, "Our parents were very close and affectionate with each other. We just saw a great marriage, so we were surprised when it finally ended."

TAKING ON TWO STATES

Tom's romance had been flourishing with his own Sue since their high-school days working part-time at a men's clothier. In early 1976 he returned to California to replace a departing manager at a store in Redwood City and Sue Casey followed him down. She landed a job at a bank in downtown San Francisco, where they lived for a while and where Tom realized he didn't really like the Golden State all that much anymore.

Nor did he enjoy the hot weather, worsened by a regional drought, and working long hours in an inferno of a store that, like all the Villages then, wasn't air-conditioned. About six months after arriving there, he had dinner with his dad, who was visiting, and announced: "I really can't stand it down here. In fact, I don't like it so much that if I can't get back to Seattle with the company, I'm just going to come back on my own." His father readily agreed to relocate him.

Tom took over the Rainier Street store, hiring new staff and making it profitable, before returning as manager to the Renton location where he'd started as a furniture pricer. He was learning that a store's success depends not on upper management but on the men and women on-site who run the business day to day:

"This business is different than most any other retail business. Every single store operates its own production facility. Target doesn't do that, K-Mart doesn't, Wal-Mart doesn't. They have distribution centers that send the merchandise to the stores. The managers have a planagram [an inventory control and merchandise display method] where they're told where to put things. In our case I really believe that it's the store manager and the production supervisor the company turns on, and everybody else should work for them. And it's the same with our team members: if we have good training, a benevolent store manager and production supervisor, we end up with stores that become like a family. Those are our successful stores. And our customers feel it."

By 1978 Tom was the district manager for stores in Spokane, Washington, Portland, Oregon, and the four then operating in California – where there was some serious patching-up to do. The lone store in Los Angeles had been run by a friend of his father, Hugh McElhenny; the two had been fraternity brothers and best men at each other's weddings. Hugh was a legendary All-America running back with the University of Washington Huskies and then became rookie of the year in the first of his thirteen seasons in the National Football League. He was named All Pro four times and later selected to the NFL Hall of Fame. But he knew nothing about the retail trade "and he had too many other interests,"," says Bill, who had the painful task of firing his buddy. ("I learned something from that," Tom says. "Which is: don't hire your friends. It's one thing if you work together and become friends, but I would not hire a friend.")

Originally, Tom was going to share the management of the California outlets with Jeff and John Bacon. "So we flew down and it's agreed that I will be the Bay-area district manager [while living in Washington], and then we went on to LA to look at that shabby old unprofitable store too. This was after Hugh had left and things were not good; management was not strong. Jeff and John both looked at each other and then at me and said, 'You know what, Tom? We think as long as you are coming to California, you probably should do this store too.' And I kept pushing back, but finally I realized they were right."

He took over a mixed bag of stores, including one in the gritty Pico Rivera area of east Los Angeles. "We couldn't believe what a dump it was. It had gone years without making money. I saw my first cockroach there, as big as a glass, running across the floor. The store was in an old boxing arena and a number of years later, we found a homeless man who'd found a way in from the outside and was living in the bleachers behind the wall near the store manager's office."

One of Tom's early tasks was trying to fix a troubled relationship with a charity called PARCA, the Peninsula Association for Retarded Children and Adults. "I had never been to a meeting with one of the not-for-profit organizations. PARCA's executive director was Shirley Bishop, who I found to be nice and refreshing. I am about twenty and she's in her late twenties (I thought she was kind of old), but we hit it off. We realized that the issue was my predecessor and her board of directors, who were at odds. What I really learned and had already seen in play with my father is to go the extra mile. Do what is necessary, do what is right – this is a nonprofit organization that is serving people. We have to lead, we have to be as generous as we can afford to be. Little stuff, like how do we treat the truck driver who's unloading at our store? And if the charity wants us to reimburse them for a certain expense that we thought was not really legit, I'd just say, 'We *will* pay for that'. And when you start to go the extra mile, then they come back the other way. We built a very strong relationship in a relatively short order."

ARRIVALS — AND AN ATTEMPTED DEPARTURE

Rod VanLeeuwen

Towards the end of the decade, there were attempts to bring more professionalism into the business. In '76 Jeff had been managing the Portland store when he hired Rod VanLeeuwen, a frat-brother friend of his from college, who'd been doing collections for a bank's credit-card business. Rod became store manager after two years and quickly adopted a new tool that the analytical John Bacon had introduced to tally and record every item at every price point that every department processed – "so we could give feedback on our own output compared to the overall quotas," Rod explains. By '81 he was running two stores, in Tacoma, Washington, and a new one in a pleasant suburb in nearby Puyallup, which was the first to be based in a building constructed especially for the company.

As the 1980s ended, an increasingly busy head office was looking for an assistant controller. In came Mike Griffith, an accountant who'd studied at the University of Washington and was an unhappy roving auditor for Sears. Thrift Village Inc. was still sending out its accounts to a service bureau rather than doing them in-house. Bill Fraser as controller was a rock-steady presence, but when Mike tried to learn the accounting system from Marie Gunn, she'd snap at him: "Why do you want to know that?" As he describes the scene, "It was just terrible, but I loved it. There were reams of paper with cigarette burns that were the general ledger. Marie would send it in with her handwritten notes and if we were real lucky, we'd get a financial statement back. I liked her because I had an aunt just like her, but it was World War III to get things changed." Eventually the company bought its first computer, a Honeywell dubbed Danno that was a so-called mini-computer, about the size of a refrigerator. And later a true mini, a $30,000 Fujitsu that demanded $5,000 in office rewiring just to operate it.

Meanwhile, George Seferos had been essentially squeezed out as general manager by the sheer presence of the family triumvirate of Tom, Jeff, and John. George promptly opened a competing thrift-store chain in

Seattle with his wife, Jackie, the manager of a Value Village in Renton, and their children. "Bill was not happy with that," says Bill Fraser.

Tom and Sue were married in 1979, but despite his rapid progress in management, he wasn't happy in the business either. "I felt I was just a cog in the wheel, I was the boss's son, and I was just generally feeling sorry for myself. But I also had ambition and I wanted to go out and start my own thing." Not long after his marriage, he approached his father to announce that he was leaving the company to open his own thrift store in Albuquerque, New Mexico. "I'd been there and thought it was a place with no competition. I expected my dad to try and talk me out of it, but I didn't expect what happened."

His father started crying, put his arms around Tom, and said, "I don't want you to leave. I want to make you the president of the company. And I'm going to arrange to sell you and Jeff and John some of the business some time down the road."

A little overwhelmed, Tom agreed to stay.

Soon after, Bill Ellison made an independent decision that would take Tom – and the company – in an altogether new direction.

North.

"Dad pushed us kicking and screaming into Canada."

O, CANADA!

CHAPTER FOUR

Bill had married again, on the rebound, to Betty Cooley. It would be a tempestuous and relatively short-lived relationship – from 1976 to 1983 – but one that affected the company's fortunes in a dramatic way. Betty was a Canadian, from Vancouver, British Columbia, and on his visits there her new husband realized that a Value Village could do well in her hometown, just a two and a half hours' drive north of Seattle. There was nothing like it in Canada and he instinctively felt the demographics of the population and the retail conditions seemed just right for such a venture. At the time, Bill never really thought beyond opening a single store in Vancouver.

Other members of the family and some of his trusted confidants rebelled against the idea. "He pushed us kicking and screaming into Canada," Tom remembers. "We thought, 'How stupid – why do we want to go there?' That is all the advice that he got from the three of us – John, Jeff, and me – and his other senior managers at the time. My rationale was that we could just open up more stores in California for a lot less administrative hassle. And it was a hard deal to get into Canada in those days. The Trudeau government was not real big on foreign investment."

When Bill first started exploring the possibility of setting up a store in Canada, he ran smack into its Foreign Investment Review Agency – FIRA – designed to limit the amount of non-Canadian control of companies operating in the country.

Opposite: Downtown Vancouver, B.C., in 1980 – a city on the verge of a big boom.

About 1978 Bill approached Laing Brown, a young lawyer of half a dozen years' experience with what was then Russell & DuMoulin, a prominent Vancouver legal firm. Laing well knew the common cynical saying: "There is nothing to fear but FIRA itself." He agreed to represent the company with the federal agency's bureaucrats in Ottawa, the Canadian capital. Meeting there with the two Bills – Ellison and Fraser, the controller – he soon sized up these thrift-store operators: "Bill Ellison was the bigger-picture guy and Bill Fraser made sure the ideas got implemented."

Bill F., who felt neutral about the concept of expanding to Canada, was overseeing the company's application, which stressed the relationship with a charitable organization. "The government was negative about it initially. We met these FIRA guys in a smoke-filled interrogation room and they thought they had all this power. They were looking for the benefits to Canada; we were guilty until proven innocent. They told us we had to have fifty-one-per-cent Canadian ownership. We said, 'No, we can't do that.'"

Laing reminisces: "Here was an American go-get-'em businessman facing all this red tape and bureaucracy and it just didn't sit well with Bill Ellison. Bill Fraser is quite an accommodating, easy-going fellow who could play that game well. He and I tried to encourage Bill to play ball with them. But they were sticking with their line in the sand."

Bill E. recalls the session as a series of gruelling questions – "like we were potential bank robbers trying to come into Canada. They were not receptive at all and after a certain point I just stood up and said, 'It's obvious that you are not interested in our coming to Canada, so if that's the way you feel about it, we are not going to come.' And we started to walk out the door until they said, 'Wait a minute, wait a minute.' That really changed the tone of the whole meeting. It's like they were testing us to see how far they could be difficult with us."

"Finally," Bill Fraser says, "we agreed to offer twenty-five per cent to local management on our terms after we got up and running. They ended up agreeing to that."

The first person to whom the two Bills offered the one-quarter ownership was Laing Brown himself. "Although I got on well with both of them, being a barrister and solicitor I said it would be a conflict of interest to be a shareholder in the company. I was more interested in acting for them as a lawyer and doing the correct thing. In retrospect, I might have been better to go into business with these guys. My wife, Kathleen, now says, 'What were you thinking?'"

Bill E. chided him, "You're so busy stopping to pick up the nickels that you're tripping over the $20 bills." But the men had formed a bond: Laing, who became a partner in Russell & DuMoulin, continues to act as the company's lawyer in many Canadian matters to this day (although with a different firm, Borden Ladner Gervais).

Bill also considered offering a quarter-share in the Canadian business to Cliff Parish, a plumber friend of Betty's family, who was hired as the original manager of the first store. Tom recalls, "John and I had nothing to do with his selection, but at that point we were the ones that were charged with trying to teach him how to run the business, and it was just not going to work." The offer to make him a partner lapsed as the government seemed to back off its legislation affecting foreign ownership. Cliff soon left to set up his own operation, called Scotty's Thrift Village. He took his store supervisor with him, Tom says, "and they got to about four or five stores and lasted for at least five or six years before they failed. They probably had the best run of any of the would-be competitors."

In setting up his first Canadian store, Bill had already found a local charity to work with. Like the people who founded the Northwest Center in Seattle, a dozen parents of children with developmental disabilities had come together in 1952 to help integrate their kids into public schools. In time, the group – then called the Vancouver-Richmond Association for Mentally Handicapped People – evolved into the largest charitable society of its kind in western Canada, now known as the Developmental Disabilities Association. Bill gave them a fifty-one-percent split of the take. Eventually the company would collaborate closely with other non-profits, among them a national charity, the Canadian Diabetes Association, which formed a symbiotic relationship that would be highly profitable for both parties.

In early 1980 Value Village Stores Ltd. was formed as a Canadian limited company in British Columbia, and the Ellison family was in high gear planning its first foray onto foreign, if friendly soil. Vancouver was a vibrant and ethnically diverse city on the verge of becoming an important international center linked to nations of the Pacific Rim.

The first Canadian store — on Hastings Street in Vancouver's yeasty east end – was almost an immediate success, prompting plans for more outlets.

Bill asked the twenty-four-year-old Rod VanLeeuwen, who was overseeing two Washington stores, "Would you consider moving to Canada?" No, but Rod *would* work in Vancouver through the week and return home on weekends. He, Tom, and John Bacon were delegated to make a store. They found a modestly sized location on Hastings Street, a main drag in the city's lower-income east end – "about as inner-city as we get," Rod says – and began building the fixtures right on site.

He was involved in hiring staff. "I was overwhelmed by the response – 400-plus applicants for a crew of about twenty. And I was impressed at the ethnic diversity. We had one Asian woman applying who under 'Sex' wrote 'No.' Clearly language was an issue."

The same pent-up flood was released in supplying the store with product. The charity had begun gathering goods from householders three months before the planned opening in April. "We learned a big lesson about starting up in an untapped market," Tom remembers. "We received so much merchandise that we overfilled the store and had to stop soliciting – there just wasn't any more room to put the stock." Rod explains: "There was nobody picking up this stuff at the customer's house – it was a totally virgin supply of fabulous material." Nine out of ten people on the charity's list put out goods for pickup, compared with six of ten in the U.S.

"We were all these wide-eyed young Americans," Tom says, "and we felt sophisticated to be in a new culture." John recalls those days as difficult: "There wasn't any way to get to Vancouver but driving back and forth from Seattle all the time, and I learned to hate that road. Then there was a whole new tax table to learn for the merchandise and certain things we had to do certain ways because of Canadian law. And where do you even get hangers? You had to find new sources, so it was absolutely starting all over again. You didn't know where you could get the best buys; it was trial and error."

John's brother, Mike, helped by organizing floor layouts, painting walls, and training new team members on how to price and merchandise. "I found Canadians very refreshing. But I viewed them as being a lot more structured and follow-the-rules than we as Americans are," he says now. "When you build a store, you're supposed to have permits, but we'd wait until we got caught. We were always looking for ways to bend the rules a little."

The grand opening of the Hastings store was not particularly impressive and the launch team was glum for the first few days about the lack of traffic. But within three months, as people came to understand what a privately run thrift store offered, the owners knew they had a winner. As Tom says, "In the thrift-store business, I would call Canada the perfect storm" – the ideal combination of elements that come together to create a mighty force. "Our mainstay clientele are middle-income people, not necessarily wealthy but not necessarily poor or low-income. Canada's middle-income as a percentage is just bigger than in the U.S. Most other American retailers have done better in Canada store for store and that's true of us. And because no one was doing a very good job recycling people's usable discards there, people were just thrilled to have someone use stuff that they were throwing away. We were also able to hire top-quality people in Canada, career-minded managers."

Not at first, however. When Cliff Parish, the store's original manager, didn't work out, the company bumped up a furniture pricer named Ray Duplessis. A French-Canadian from Sherbrooke, Quebec, he had long since lived on the west coast and would become a fixture with Value Village over the years, eventually returning to his home province as district manager. And when the first manager of the charity's collection service in Vancouver didn't survive, the association's executive director and Rod hired Wayne Penner, a Canadian who'd lived in England most of his young life. He'd since returned to Canada, where he worked for a government unemployment-insurance office in Vancouver. Wayne would have a lengthy career with the company

Ray proved to be an efficient manager and when the second Canadian operation opened in 1981, he was transferred to run the store in the Greater Vancouver city of Surrey, with a population that had grown by more than fifty per cent in the past decade. The timing was perfect: the community, running from the Fraser River to the American border, was on the cusp of a boom that would double the head-count over the next two decades and turn it into British Columbia's second-largest center after Vancouver. Ray's wife, Anne, had worked for a major jewelry store and came on as a temporary sorter in Surrey, became a production supervisor, and then stayed with the company for years in various roles.

CHRIS AND SCOTT AND MIKE AND SHANNON

Over the next couple of years, Value Villages opened in Haney and Langley, two smaller communities along the Fraser River just east of Vancouver. Chris Barton, a commercial real-estate broker in Vancouver, had heard the Ellisons were looking for properties and arranged to show Tom, Jeff, and John what he remembers as "three lousy choices." One of them was in Haney. "We stopped for lunch there and I took them to a Burger King – they still kid me about that." They did the deal within a couple of weeks and Chris was soon their exclusive Canadian agent. "I found the guys like young whippersnappers – a little cocky. Tom was the leader of the three and his father was the statesman. For John and Jeff, business wasn't the be-all and end-all. Jeff was the laid-back Californian."

Rod VanLeeuwen became district manager for the three Canadian outlets (as well as the stores in Seattle). When he moved on to be a one-man planning and development manager for all the company's operations, Jeff began overseeing Canada.

At the time, he'd been running a new enterprise that his father had identified during the global energy crunch of the late 1970s. A company called Buck Stove, born in the Blue Ridge Mountains of North Carolina, offered a line of free-standing, wood-burning fireplace inserts. Bill Ellison became the Pacific Northwest franchisee for the stoves and added Hunter ceiling fans and other products to sell in a few stores he'd opened.

Buck Stove Northwest preoccupied both Bill and Jeff. By now, Scott Blomquist, Jeff's high-school buddy, had joined the company. A Mormon, he'd travelled through the Middle East and Europe and did missionary work in Ecuador after high school. In 1980, after graduating in communications from Brigham Young University, he began working for the Ellisons as their first, one-man advertising and marketing department. ("Somebody had told Bill that he should hire some Mormons because they're honest and hard-working," Scott recalls. "I said I was just an ordinary person.")

He was soon struck by the current rift in the company: "The thrift business then wasn't glamorous to anyone but Tom and John. The first couple of years I was there, eighty per cent of the conversation around the staff table with Bill was centered around Buck Stoves. Then we became national distributor for a portable interior home heater from Sweden and I travelled to trade shows and worked with Jeff to set up dealers. Most months we were losing money. Meanwhile, the thrift stores in the background were making a lot. In hindsight, it was a bad way to run a business. Fortunately, a year or two later we decided to focus on the thrift stores." The failing Buck Stoves franchise was wound down.

That's when Jeff started making trips north to direct Canadian operations. One of his key managers was twenty-seven-year-old Mike Davison, who at a tender eighteen had successfully run a shoe store in competition with his father, whose own business went bankrupt. Mike had been a management trainee under Ray Duplessis and, with his solid retail background, learned fast. Looking at the racks of men's, women's, and children's shoes, he remarked, "Ray, do you know how hard it is for people to find a pair of shoes when we don't size them?" Ray told him it was corporate policy not to arrange footwear by size. Then Mike and another trainee were sent to head office in Renton to shadow two crack managers: Tony DiMaina, then running the store in Burien, and Don

The creative Mike Davison began his career at the Hastings store and went on to introduce innovations to the company that became his legacy.

Pingree, in charge of another in the Seattle suburb of Lynnwood. Don, who'd been a western manager for Spalding USA, asked Mike to suggest how he could improve the store's stagnating shoe sales.

"Size your shoes, man," Mike said.

"Brilliant idea," Don replied.

"But they won't let you do that."

"Who's 'they?'" Don countered, forever endearing himself to Mike. And that was the birth of shoe-sizing in Value Villages.

Returning to the Hastings store, Mike noticed that the pricers in the Back Room were sorting out and saving the best merchandise – anything new or of name-brand quality – to buy for themselves instead of putting it out on the sales floor. "So I invented the twenty-four-hour rule: Employees cannot buy anything until it has been out on the floor for twenty-four hours, so the customers get first crack at it. Well, as soon as we put that rule in place, customer frequency increased and sales shot up instantly." It's a rule that still exists in the company to this day.

"Tom Ellison and, before him, WOE" – as Mike calls Bill familiarly – "were huge believers in unleashing people and letting them exhibit their talents. Over the years, what was demonstrated to them in this company is if you unleash people to their potential, everybody wants to do good and will exceed your expectations."

Mike Davison's creative thinking encouraged the company to put him in charge of the new outlet in Langley, a city that had grown in population by more than fifty per cent in a decade. But first he and Rod had to transform it from a thick-beamed, concrete-walled supermarket space to a thrift store. "Back then we didn't have a construction company and so it was hard hat, boots, crowbars, peeling stuff off the walls, laying floor tiles. You just go in and tear it apart. We had contractors to build for us, but we went in and did the demolition."

Two of the people who worked for Mike in Langley would become key figures in Value Village Stores and what became Savers Inc. His first production supervisor, Brenda Campbell, went on to help Mike launch a new operation in Nanaimo, on Vancouver Island (and most recently was a manager in Chilliwack, east of Vancouver). The other woman whose long career with the company had its first real start in Langley was Shannon Vernerey – or Givens, as she was then.

Shannon, a Saskatchewan farmer's daughter, had bought her own beauty salon at nineteen and ran it for seven years in Saskatoon before loading her worldly goods into her Mustang GTO and moving to Vancouver in early 1985. By chance, while she was looking for work, she wandered into her first Value Village store with her sister, who bought a toy snake for fifteen cents. About a week later, she answered a help-wanted ad for a company called TVI – which a year earlier had become the new name of Thrift Village Inc. She didn't know TVI owned this strange, snake-selling store she'd visited and she didn't know that the low-key, down-to-earth young fellow who interviewed her, Jeff Ellison, was the founder's son.

She became a management trainee in the fourth Canadian store to open, in the Greater Vancouver city of New Westminster, but the acting manager there had her doing nothing but price women's clothes for the first month. When Ray then met with her and found how little she'd had a chance to learn about the business, he began training her, asking a lot of

Shannon Givens, a Saskatchewan farmer's daughter, was the company's second female manager and soon became a district manager in Canada.

"why" questions: "*Why* are you pricing this item at that figure?" Eventually he put her in charge of a week-long sale, which was so successful that he presented her with a dozen roses (and let the acting manager go).

Shannon was soon transferred to help open the Langley store that Mike Davison was managing. Ray Duplessis's wife, the knowledgeable and dedicated Anne Duplessis, who had once been production supervisor there, came back to teach her about miscel – jewelry and all the other miscellaneous merchandise besides clothing, furniture, and books. After less than a year in Langley, Shannon worked briefly at the Hastings operation before being moved to run the store in Haney. She was the second female manager, in charge of the smallest outlet in the chain. While she introduced some innovations – a fashion show, with a stage the staff and their husbands built – her major *aha!* was the simple realization that the more product the charity trucks brought in, the more profit the store could earn.

"I would stay in the store and accept trucks late in the day. I can remember crawling over furniture to close the loading-bay door to lock up at night because the Back Room was so small. If I turned anything down, I kept thinking of lost sales so I would take everything and anything. I actually increased the quota substantially, by about a couple of hundreds OKs while I was there. That was unheard-of at that time, but the sales went up and people were taking note of what was happening. I worked a lot more just on the tactical side of getting more merchandise in the store. The managers had a lot of autonomy; no one told me I could *not* do that."

It was a lesson she would take with her as she progressed quickly up the ranks in Canada. Mike Davison by then had launched the company's largest outlet, in south Vancouver, and when he reluctantly became district manager for the burgeoning B.C. operation, Shannon took over managing that store. It was losing money consistently and her first attempts at working with the employees there were ill-fated. "I had a store that was stuffed to the rafters with product in the Back Room and I was working my staff pretty hard. I had some high expectations and I was pushing them past their limits. They went over my head and called Mike and he had a conversation with me. I had some issues with Mike that I had to work myself through, too. But I went back to the team more with the attitude that we needed to figure out how to work together. I'd just totally forgot all about the people side of the business. It was a great lesson: you spend more time with the people you work with than you do with your own family. So to build the relationship, I put a lot of focus on the team and involved them in the plan for the store."

She developed a strong management group, which allowed her to spend more time with the solicitation manager of the charity supplying her product. It was only the second non-profit the Canadian stores were dealing with, a local branch of what was then the loosely organized Canadian Diabetes Association. "She and I would sit down and go through the profit-and-loss and figure out how we could cut her costs," Shannon says. "It took us about six or seven months before her side was not eating all my profit and we started to get the store profitable."

COLD, WARM ALBERTA

The south Vancouver store opened in April 1986. It was the sixth in the Lower Mainland of B.C., where the forthcoming Expo 86, the world exposition, was generating excitement about the Greater Vancouver area and the province as a whole. Caught up in their own success there, the Ellisons realized they had a formula that would play well in the other nine provinces of Canada. In '85 their first target had been neighboring Alberta, where they had to decide whether to locate in the petroleum center of Calgary or the provincial capital of Edmonton. While Jeff was the Canadian operations director, Tom was in charge of finding the right location for a store and a local charity as a partner. They found a decent store location in Edmonton.

"I had never been that far east or north," Tom says. "We went there in February and I didn't bring a coat" – and Edmonton is notorious for its arctic-like winter climate. All he had was a sport jacket to wear to his meeting with Reg Peters, who was a legendary executive director of the Alberta Association for Community Living (AACL), which served children and adults with developmental disabilities. "And in that weather we had to walk about six blocks from our hotel. I was a dumb twenty-seven-year-old."

Not so dumb that he hadn't prepared for the meeting. "Reg was serving on the board of Goodwill Industries of Edmonton at the time and we told him our story. Reg hadn't known anything about us, but the people at the Vancouver-Richmond Association for the Mentally Handicapped had told him what we were doing for them.

"Reg learned about us and became a believer, so he let Goodwill in Edmonton know that he was going to resign from the board because he was afraid that it would be a conflict. And the day before we opened in Edmonton, Goodwill did a press release saying we were this American for-profit company coming to town and were going to steal all of the money out of their coffers. Keep in mind that at this time, if you wanted to give your used clothes to Goodwill, mostly they wouldn't accept it at their stores because they were so full. And in those days, they picked up at your house, but you had to book six to eight weeks in advance. They just had so much stuff that they couldn't be bothered and so the public was throwing things away.

"We opened the Edmonton store the day after the *Edmonton Sun* had carried a semi-controversial article about us – and we had the biggest opening in our history." And, as it turned out, Reg became one of Value Village's strongest champions as the profit AACL made from the relationship transformed it from a provincial organization that had to charge its local branches dues to one that gave money back to them in grants.

Tom recalls, "When we opened that store, I was so excited that I couldn't sleep all night long. I could see all these stores across the country. I started talking that way: 'Let's open more stores, this is such an opportunity, why don't we just crank it up?'" But his brother, Jeff, had a different vision of his own future. "He wasn't interested in being part of the team that had to deliver that growth."

Jeff's declaration would change the lives and fortunes of the two brothers before the 1980s came to a close.

"We knew we needed a new name and had to brand it. 'Savers' works really well."

GROWING UP

CHAPTER FIVE

From early on, Bill Ellison believed in the wisdom of sharing the wealth – not only with his non-profit partners but also with the people who worked for him. When Tony DiMaina was a manager in the 1970s, he began earning a bonus of ten per cent of the bottom line if his operation was profitable – an incentive for him (and other store managers at the time) that increased by another percentage point over each of the next five years. Later Bill arranged for Tony to borrow $10,000 from the company to buy twenty per cent of the property housing the Burien, Washington, store; today, he reaps about $40,000 a year from his investment. In 1978, when Bill bought the Redwood City, California, store location from the landlord, he made controller Bill Fraser and general manager George Seferos partners in the deal. After giving him down payments, they paid for each of their twenty-four-per-cent shares in the store out of its cashflow. This philosophy of splitting up the spoils would continue through the years with various systems of bonuses and profit-sharing for managers and their team members.

Over the last decade, however, the corporate mindset changed. "My dad has always had a saying: 'If you pay peanuts, you get monkeys,'" Tom says. "What he was driving home was 'Don't be cheap. Pay people generously, treat them like they are a great asset to the business – and they will become one.' I believe that when store managers had a bigger piece of the action, they were definitely more owners as opposed to managers of the business. Tony was an owner and the company succeeded. What happens

Opposite: Savers became the name for stores in new U.S. markets beyond the west coast.

In 1985 Savers moved its corporate headquarters – the store support center, as it came to be called – to beautiful Bellevue, Washington's fourth-largest center.

is when you share a bigger piece of the pie, the pie gets bigger. I really believe that. It creates loyalty and longevity, which for the most part is good. But the genesis of changing our bonus plan was that we couldn't get people to leave their stores. If we were really going to grow, we wanted to move people up to district managers and regional managers. We wanted people to have ambition to go to different cities with us – but sometimes they were doing so well with one store that they wouldn't move.

"The other thing was that the store managers were so focused on the bottom line that they wouldn't spend money on their stores. And some of them didn't want to pay the charities what we should pay them. That was wrong because the charities played a very big part in our success. So all those things combined to make us rethink our compensation plan.... If I was doing it again, I would personally choose to compensate people very well on the bonus side. But the company now is different than it was in a lot of ways." Yet even today, the nearly 350 managers – of the 200 stores, the districts and regions, and human resources, loss prevention, field support, and the store support center in Bellevue – have been given stock options in Savers and recently received unexpected dividends when the company was refinanced.

Back in 1983, when Bill was calling the shots in a much-smaller company, bonuses were more generous and managers had a chance of becoming partners in certain corporate ventures. That year, his personal universe changed when he and Betty divorced and she began to open a series of stores in Toronto, called Thrift Villa, all of which went out of business. His second failed marriage seemed to make Bill increasingly conscious of the importance of family. A year later he decided it was time to invite his two sons and his son-in-law to become partners. "He made it really easy on us," Tom says. "He did a contract of sales with us, with no money down, and then we just paid him out of our share of the cash flow – if there was any – over many years. He sold us each sixteen per cent – about fifty per cent of the business. That's how generous the guy is. You know, he didn't need to. In hindsight he was brilliant for doing it because he lit a fuse. I don't think we would have had the interest to do what we did otherwise – to build the company to the size that it became. He did it because he wanted to share the family business with us."

"I think we all looked at it as an opportunity," John Bacon agrees. "At that time Bill was there, but he was not there – in the sense that he did not have the motivation to want to build things himself. So when he said, 'Okay, you guys get a piece of this,' that's giving you some account-ability to make something of yourself. Bill was always pretty generous in that regard. It was the same philosophy that I believed in, too, which was if you give people a piece of the action, they are going to succeed, and if you don't . . . . "

By then Bill Ellison was actively involved again with Alcoholics Anonymous, and through mutual friends had met the elegant-looking Carole (Haas) LaFollette, who was raised on a farm in Washington's Yaki-ma Valley. A decade younger than he is, she was a graduate of the Univer-sity of Washington in home-economics business and had lived with her first husband, a son, and a daughter in California – where she worked for a small-town newspaper as a food columnist and even set type and sold ads. Moving back to Seattle, Carole was divorced and for eighteen months became a secretary for the famed Hollywood director Stanley Kramer, then making a film locally. She was doing secretarial work for lawyers when Bill began dating her. They married in 1985, in a meaningful union that endures to this day. (And when she and her husband's first wife,

Bill Ellison met Carole LaFollette, a farmer's daughter from the Yakima Valley, when she was a legal secretary in Seattle; they were married in 1985.

Sue, met at Tom's thirtieth birthday party, Carole said, "If we hadn't been married to the same man at different times, we might have been good friends." Sue replied, "Don't let that get in our way." And they didn't.)

Happily remarried, Bill now had even more reason to pass the day-to-day of business on to the younger generation. "My father was great at delegating and then stepping aside to let us accomplish the task," Tom adds. "He never second-guessed us, even when we made mistakes."

The trio signaled their new responsibilities by wearing a sports coat or suit and tie to work every day. In '85 they moved corporate head-quarters from the crowded Renton location to roomy new digs in the city where the family was living: Bellevue. Just three miles east of Seattle, it was rapidly evolving from a bedroom community to a prosperous and pleasant center of 117,000, the state's fourth-largest. The modern office building just happened to be next door to the Bellevue Club, where the Ellisons were members.

Emboldened by their fresh financial involvement, Tom and John in particular began to propel the expansion that saw TVI more than triple in size over the next ten years. Jeff, however, felt less of a commitment to the business. "I think deep down in my heart I knew that one day Jeff would leave," his dad says now. "Jeff was not suited for the drive [to build the company]. He is easy-going and caring. He's a beautiful guy and everyone he meets, he charms. In contrast with Tom, who just charges like a bull straight ahead."

Tom: "Jeff has been more driven by arts and by music than he has by business. He is a very gregarious, personable guy but never enjoyed the grind of people management. Moreover, he did not like to travel. The company was configured so that I looked after real estate and all of our partner relationships, and to some degree pushed growth, while Jeff looked after Canada and John the U.S."

Shannon Vernerey remembers that when she was running a store in Maple Ridge, B.C., Jeff's visits were remarkably low-key: "He used to tell me that he came out to make himself feel good because the store was running so well. We would walk around the store and talk about a few things and then he would take me for lunch. But anytime I had a question, I could call him and he always responded quickly. He was a really nice man to work for."

Mike Davison, recalling his time as a new manager in the first Langley, B.C., location, describes a typical visit that had Jeff driving up from Bellevue in his Range Rover with a mountain bike in the back. After looking around the store, Jeff would ask, "Everything going good?" and, hearing that things were fine, said, "Well, good, I'm going to unload my bike and ride over to the Haney store and across on the Albion ferry."

"Jeff, wait a minute."

"You said everything was good."

"Well, it is, but you need to pay me more money."

"Okay, how much do you want?"

And Mike says he received the raise he requested.

While Jeff oversaw operations in Canada, Tom was traveling across the country to find real estate for new stores and to sign up charity partners. The Edmonton location was followed by a second a year later, in 1986, and then in the following two years by outlets in the thriving oil capital of Calgary and the first in the east – in the Quebec metropolis of Montreal, Canada's second-largest city and, with a largely French-speaking population, one of its most spirited.

Tom traveled with Chris Barton, the Vancouver property broker. "Chris came along with us on that first trip to Toronto and Montreal," he says. "The idea was to pick a city to grow in next, and in 1987 Toronto was just on fire while Montreal wasn't. We could have gone either way, but in Toronto we couldn't afford the real estate."

As Chris says, "Montreal was a bit depressed in those days and I knew the city, growing up there, and knew the French-Canadian culture. My family had got into retail with a clothing store right downtown." So Montreal was the choice to begin expanding into eastern Canada. "The first property deal was in the west end, an area in transition from industrial. It was in an old soft-drink bottling plant and had a very tough landlord – so tough that when we asked to put an antenna on the roof to receive music, they said no, not unless we rented part of the roof." The westerners frequented a nearby restaurant that featured a magician called Tom au Magique, a nickname that soon stuck to Tom Ellison whenever he visited Quebec.

Ray Duplessis – who'd transferred from Vancouver to take charge of the Alberta operation – was now tapped to move back to his home province as manager of a store known by the French-language translation Village des Valeurs. Although Ray's Québécois French was a little rusty, Tom had absolutely no knowledge of the language as he negotiated a contract in French with a charity serving the mentally disabled.

Shannon, who came to help for the week of the grand opening in 1988, reminisces: "I don't speak French fluently and so that was a bit of a struggle, although everyone in the area was very fluent in English. For the opening we had huge customer counts, but our noon reading that first day was very low and everybody was really nervous. And then the night sales for Day One were about $10,000 from six to nine P.M., which was huge and unheard of.

"Everyone in the province smokes and all the customers had cigarettes hanging out of their mouths; we were constantly asking people to put them out. In other provinces, if people drop something, they pick it up and put it back. In Montreal that did not happen. The first day when we closed, Anne Duplessis and I took about thirty shopping carts up and down the aisles to pick things up. It was like a bomb hit that sales floor. And this may be a cultural thing in Quebec, but a lot of customers then didn't want people to know that they were shopping thrift, so they'd bring their own bags that didn't have our name on them. Today it's a different story."

When Tom and Chris checked the addresses on the sales receipts after the opening, they were surprised that so many customers lived in the tony English-speaking enclave of Westmount.

Two years later, the company launched two more Villages in Montreal and through the 1990s a string of other stores throughout the province: Quebec City, Trois Rivières, Laval, Ste Foy, Montreal North, Gatineau, and Longueuil (the newest, on Montreal's West Island, opened in 2001). Ray Duplessis eventually became district manager for Quebec. He recalls a time when a language barrier intruded, even though both parties were speaking French. A pricer in the Back Room of a new store asked him where she should put a rack of ties ready for sale. He told her they should go on the floor and be color-coded. A little while later a bewildered production supervisor asked Ray to come out to the sales floor and see what had happened.

"When I walked out of the production door," he says, "to my amazement the ties were all very nicely laid down – literally on the floor, all color-coded. It made for a nice carpet, but not quite what I had in mind."

THE DEAL-MAKER

The man who had closed the leasing deal on the first Montreal store was a freshman with the company, although he was often in contact with Tom before coming aboard in 1987. After Walter Scott graduated from Virginia's Washington and Lee University with an economics degree, he'd taken a high-paid job working on an oil-drilling platform off Houston. When the petroleum boom waned, Walt became a leasing agent (with no previous experience) for Jerry J. Moore, a legendary private developer of strip shopping malls throughout Texas. His job included cold-calling thrift-store owners, which is how he met Tom, trying to interest him in two store sites in a depressed area of Houston. Tom told the agent, "We'd never lease space in these low-income, nondescript centers."

"Which stunned me," Walt recalls. "Tom had already realized that the best customer was a middle- to upper-income female with two or more kids at home." That was in '85, and for the next couple of years he kept badgering Tom – who finally asked, "If I offer you a job, will you stop calling me?"

Walt's first assignment as director of real estate was completing the deal for the Victoria store, the largest in the chain, and then he went on to negotiate agreements for sites in Coquitlam, B.C., and Montreal. He agrees with Chris Barton about the tough Québécois landlord: "We called him Dr. No. He tore us apart on the lease. It took forever to do it." Walt, however, was a quick study and soon understood the strengths and weaknesses of his new employer. "I realized that from the deals they'd been doing, their footprint was good, but their control wasn't." By "footprint," he means the locations the company chose, which were mostly ranked a solid "B-plus." They were usually on busy streets, where shoppers felt comfortable, and near enough to – but not within – good shopping malls with their high rents.

Walt became responsible for deal-making on sites throughout North America. Once when they were considering a location, Tom said, "It's kind of thin on population, Walt."

"But it's growing real fast."

"Here's what I think about that," Tom said. "Pioneers get the arrows, settlers get the land."

In other words, Walt sums up, "wait till enough people move there before putting a store there."

But in the early days of his career, the company wasn't carefully controlling its future on even the good sites: "They were doing only five-year leases with five-year options." Renewing them, he negotiated ten-year leases with four- to five-year options. "The options are where the money is – by that time you've trained customers to come to the store. We also realized that our customers were very loyal; we didn't have to be in A-#1 locations. We had a good concept, but landlords gave us no respect – like Rodney Dangerfield. Some of them would just flat out hang up when we called because they had such a prejudice against thrift stores. I told them,

'You're not our target customers. They're the people who work for you, with middle incomes.'" He sold the landlords on a win-win-win proposition: "We recycle all the stuff that would normally go to a landfill; a hundred per cent of our cost of goods goes to non-profit organizations; and we make a profit."

Pointing out how entrepreneurial the company was then, he says, "We'd lease a location without knowing if we could rezone it or get a variance real fast." Sometimes Walt, Tom, and Rod had to appear at council meetings in an attempt to change zoning regulations. "We realized reputation and image was important, so we'd wear ties even if the councillors were wearing jeans." In 1988 they rented a fleabag hotel room in Winnipeg, Manitoba, and flipped a coin to see which of them got to sleep there while the other two appeared before the city council at an unholy 1 A.M. Rod won the toss, but Walt and Tom figured he really lost because he had to stay in the grimy room. (Years later, when Walt was scouting New York for sites, he finally found a hotel with a vacancy late one evening. "Do you want it by the hour or the night?" the desk clerk asked. That's when Walt noticed all the women sitting around the lobby.)

Eventually, as vice-president of real estate, Walt set up a system for rigid oversight of the occupancy costs of their leases – those so-called uncontrollable expenses levied by landlords. "Over time, we had three 'lease police' – accountants on commission to tear apart the landlords' occupancy-cost statements." About half their audits found errors or wilful fabrications – such as a landlord's pleasure-boat trip charged to Value Village or $80,000 the company paid in water bills over several years, which the property-owner claimed he'd paid. "Probably, including tax, we were saving about half a million dollars a year."

As Tom has described Walt Scott, "He's a dogged negotiator. He just goes to the mat on every deal on behalf of the company. His single purpose is carving out the very best deal for the business. He could retire on a particular deal and get it signed up early and make life a lot simpler for him. But what he's done is create value for the company in getting very long-term deals with options at specified rents that inure to our benefit for years to come."

NEW NAME, NEW BRAND

By the time the Montreal Village opened in 1988, Tom had been president of the company for the past year. Dubbed the heir apparent by his dad, he seemed the obvious choice, as Bill Fraser points out: "Tom came on strong. He ended up in conflicts with Jeff and John because he had confidence in what he believed and didn't necessarily agree with them on everything. During the '80s he was pushing the growth. We'd have staff meetings every week. Bill would listen to Tom and defer to him over time. Bill wasn't willing to work as hard and be there as much – letting Tom call the shots."

As Tom took over, there were twelve Canadian and twenty-eight American stores generating $40 million in annual sales. One early decision Tom made as president – along with others, especially John Bacon – was to change the names of the company's outlets in the U.S.: "In '88, when we could see that we were really going to start big growth, we had a contest to come up with a name for our expansion markets. At that time we were entering both Minnesota and Arizona and had to name stores. Ironically, in Minnesota the charity that we selected had their own thrift store and it was called Value Village. So we knew that we needed to get a new name and had to trademark that name – brand it. My personal assistant, Andrea Grad, won a thousand dollars for coming up with the name Savers. It works really well, and it was only clouded a bit at the time because one of the original Costco-type companies was called Price Savers, but it quickly went out of business. So Savers is unique." Within a few years, the company itself would be officially renamed from the ambiguous TVI to the more dynamic Savers Inc.

A year after his brother became president, Jeff announced he was formally leaving the business. He and Sandy, the high-school sweetheart who became his wife, moved with their two children to Maui, where today they live on a ranch while he pursues his musical passions and his own real-estate brokerage. (In 1989 Savers opened its first store in Hawaii with the Big Brothers Big Sisters charity. Bill Ellison had wanted to locate in the Pacific paradise for fifteen years: "It was my pleasure to try and deliver something that was a dream of his," Tom says.)

The year Jeff left, John Bacon was bumped up to executive vice-president of the company. The promotion reflected the good work he'd already done in guiding the development of the American stores and the promise of many more to come.

"The titles didn't mean a whole lot," he says, "and my commitment did not really change. I oversaw operations and the people responsible for that: all the district managers, division managers, other vice-presidents reporting to me. Tom was essentially involved with the real-estate aspect of things and the non-profits. That's not to say that he was not also involved in planning. He just wasn't hands-on day to day."

John brought his sensibility and sense of detail to his work. "My dad always used to say that it doesn't take any more effort to do it right the first time. The fact that we bought chrome clothing racks didn't cost us any more money [compared to bringing in welders to make angle-iron racks on site]. And we started buying in quantity and reduced our costs and the time it took to open new stores because we had less manufacturing to do. Again, color and style does not cost you any money. So we tried to stay current. I remember K-Marts and Targets were going through a big transition at that time, and so we did the same and came up with a new color palette and sign design."

In effect, with new furnishings, modern-looking interior signage, and the eye-catching red-and-white exterior signs, John was branding the stores. "It was always an evolutionary process to try to re-assess how to better market our product. We started doing more calculations of what was selling best and how we could better market that to the customer, what we could put in the front of the stores as opposed to the back. And these were all things that I'd learn from going to other stores and talking to people – and I'd encourage everybody to do that. Essentially, you need to use other people's brains and the most successful people don't care about you stealing their ideas. Because if you're good enough, you're going to be different enough."

More stores had been opening in Washington, Oregon, California – and in 1987 the first outside the contiguous states, in Anchorage, Alaska (which sold more than 600,000 pieces of women's clothing in its first six months). But what evolved a year later was a whole new type of retail outlet: the thrift *department* store. Although the first outlet to be named

Savers opened in St. Paul, Minnesota, in July 1988, the real flowering of the concept occurred three months later with the launch of a Savers store in Phoenix, Arizona. This 32,000-square-foot giant (about double the size of the traditional store) repositioned the company in the marketplace. As Tom described these superstores to the media then, "They're designed to be more of a regional magnet. They look very much like a nice off-price store." They did, with their brighter blues and fashionable greys and department-store fixtures replacing the homemade pegboard wall racks. "It's an unglamorous business, but our unwritten mission is to change that attitude."

Sales at the Phoenix store were soon "going like gangbusters," the thirty-two-year-old president reported. A little surprisingly, given all the competition in the alluring Sunbelt center, the state's capital and largest city. "The Southwest in general – Arizona, Nevada, New Mexico, California – have been good markets for us. People really like second-hand shopping there." The first Savers opened in Minnesota the same year Phoenix did. "Arizona had lots of privately operated thrift stores and Goodwills, Salvation Armies, St. Vincent de Pauls. We partnered with Big Brothers Big Sisters in Phoenix and they had a very tough time finding their way in the first year and getting people to donate to them because people didn't lack for places to give away used clothing. But within three years or so we dominated that market – and that's something I am very proud of. We opened up big, bright beautiful stores and people had never seen anything like them there before, so they just gravitated right to them. In Minnesota, at that time, there were virtually no thrift-store operators other than some little Goodwills, and it just took people a long time to catch on, although Minnesota is now a very strong market for us. We are still growing there and we will open up more and more stores there in the next couple of years."

"Competition never really scared us," John adds, "and it always served us better. Whenever we went into a market where there was no competition, it took us longer to get rolling just because people don't know who or what you are – versus going into an area with stores already there and you can get a jumpstart."

Mike Griffith, from his vantage point as controller, would sometimes be on a plane with John flying to stores across the continent: "John would get out the P&Ls [profit-and-loss statements] and go through every line, trying to figure out how to save $10. I'd have a couple of pads of things to follow up on."

Throughout the 1980s Mike Bacon, John's brother, had been upwardly mobile in the company. At the beginning of the decade, he'd become manager of a new store in Renton, built in a strip mall on the site of the original location. "Now I was involved in everything from the demolition to the floor plan to setting up the fixtures. That set the path for me to get involved in the company growth and help do the setups from the ground floor up." By 1983 he was a district manager of seventeen stores in the Puget Sound area while spending some time in Canada assisting Rod VanLeeuwen.

Mike collaborated in opening the landmark Phoenix store with his brother and a production supervisor then named Sue Hoss (who later married a Savers construction manager, Tim Fish). Sue hired and trained teams to work in the Back Room. "We had a lot of challenges with that first store. We'd get it laid out and get production going and then John would show up and say, 'Hmmm, I don't really think I like the ladies' department on this side of the store.' So we'd make that change and a week later, when furniture was coming out of our ears, he'd say, 'I think the furniture department should be over there.' That was a breaking point for Sue and me and we put our foot down.

"On the grand opening day, it poured like never before. The streets were flooded and the airport was closed. Needless to say, the store didn't have the big impact it could have. But its eventual success triggered us to say this was a strong, growing market. It was where we wanted to be. Today, we're sitting with thirteen stores in Arizona – and it's our best market, except for Hawaii, which has only three stores." (When the Mesa, Arizona, store launched in 1990, it wasn't water but heat that was the challenge: on the June opening day, the temperature hit 122.)

As a district manager, Mike was always tight with his managers, bouncing ideas off veterans like Tony DiMaina and Don Pingree, who was running the Lynnwood, Washington, operation. "Tony was a great guy to work with: you could let the rope out with him and only occasionally yank it back." Don, who'd been the Northwest regional manager for Spalding USA, fled the formal corporate life for the relaxed atmosphere of

The Redmond, Washington, store opened in 1984 in a community that was set to explode economically with computer-based companies like Microsoft.

a Value Village. "He was a maverick: you'd give him direction on changing a floor layout, but he'd have it his own way. Whether I agreed or not, I always had a deal that we agreed to disagree. He'd try to bend the rules and I'd have to come and give him a gentle kick. And Tom and John would say, 'You've got to push back.' Mike Davison [overseeing stores in B.C.] was another one who had a tendency to push the button too far. But God bless the guy, he made the company a lot of money. Talk about an outside thinker. We need people like that who work outside the box. If you have nothing but yes-men out there, you're not going to grow. Don Pingree was always looking for ways to improve our processes."

Mike Griffith describes Mike Bacon as "a soldier who ran a lot of stores as a manager, was a district and regional manager, and trained and grew people. And he opened a lot of stores. Camping out in a foreign city for four or five months is gruelling. Mike learned from John how to be a real profit monster. And he hasn't an enemy in the world."

CAPTIVATING CUSTOMERS,
PLEASING EMPLOYEES

One of John Bacon's friends and allies in the company was another proponent of innovation: Scott Blomquist, who since 1980 had been focused on
advertising and marketing. When he'd started, "Value Village stores were
doing little sales flyers," he recollects. "There wasn't any branding or con-
sistency from one store to the next. Both John and Bill Ellison had a high
regard for the role of advertising. But even to this day, I don't think Tom
feels there's a strong need for it if you have great product for great prices
– and that's accurate."

In Tom's own words: "I think that if we do our jobs well, we don't
need to advertise, for the most part. Costco has grown tremendously
without advertising. They have value propositions the customer wants/
needs/likes and they deliver consistently. Anybody in any business is
going to tell you that more than seventy per cent of new customers come
from word of mouth and that it is the best form of advertising you can
get. That said, for a lot of years I was happy to spend a good deal of our
budget on television. I don't believe much in anything but television for
the thrift-store business."

Scott had begun by improving the look of the flyers, window ban-
ners, and interior signage. Early on, he also saw a need for reaching out to
new customers. "John's forté was making the stores look more professional. At one meeting, I said we really ought to reposition our thrift stores.
All of the stores then were located in lower-income neighborhoods. My
thinking was that if we dressed them up and organized them better to
John's vision – and put them in suburbs or at least removed them from
the lower-income areas – I believed we could attract the middle class." He
plumped for better-looking dressing rooms and for allowing refunds. ("In
the past, if you bought it, you were stuck with it.")

Among the first departures had been the store that opened in
1984 in a suburban strip mall of middle-income Redmond. To support
the launch, he used offbeat television and radio advertising. "I thought
because we were a thrift store, we could have a little fun. We didn't have
to worry about image like Nordstrom. We'd advertise sale days – fifty per
cent off everything – and have a TV commercial about a guy camping out

the night before next to the front door of the store, waiting for the great bargains. He had a little Bunsen burner and was eating a can of beans as he talked."

Following up these ads within a couple of years were generic, institutional-type commercials based on comparative shopping. One showed a woman in front of a bifold-door closet, half of it hung with two or three items that she could buy for $50 at a regular department store and the other half bursting with clothes that she got for the same amount at Value Village. The kicker is that she pulls a dress from one half and then a second from the other side – and they're identical. Another, more controversial spot featured a heavy-set, jolly local comedienne whose daughter, a fanatical Village shopper, had tried and failed to get her mom to join her at the store. Then one day she went and was hooked – except she insisted on going incognito, in disguise, so no one would know she was shopping for clothes for her work. That commercial prompted irate calls from regular customers, who asked Scott: "Is is so bad to rub shoulders with us?"

As well as taking care of shoppers' needs, Scott was intent on improving the employees' lot. In the early '80s he was involved with small retreat-style meetings at Bill Ellison's home on Lake Washington. Initially held for managers of the troubled Buck Stoves outlets, they developed into gatherings for Value Village management. "The first of what I would call a retreat was at a resort at Hood Canal in Washington. I organized it for about thirty people. We had some training. Bill gave a speech on how the company was doing, along with reports by other key individuals, and then we had a workshop or two, dinners, and some fun and games, like golf." For one early retreat, Bill hired a powerful motivational speaker from Seattle named Lou Tice, who'd founded The Pacific Institute, an international corporation specializing in performance improvement and professional growth. "In 1983," Scott says, "we went to San Diego and next to Mexico and then it started getting bigger. 'Hey, let's go to exotic places where our managers and their spouses can't afford to go on their own – places like the Caribbean.'

"Our budgets probably started at no more than $500 per person and then ended up being close to $2,000 per person and there might be 300 people. That is big money, but we felt it was well worth every penny of it. It was a great way, from Bill's perspective, of paying tribute to the

Managers' and supervisors' retreats would grow from modest affairs in the 1980s to major events like this one in Las Vegas in 2003, with celebrity impersonators and (back row, left to right) Sandy Slater, Sean Minnick, Ian Forrester, Sam Guillemette and (front row) Stan Siudy.

employees and making sure that they feel appreciated and giving them the tools to do the job. He and the Ellisons in general wanted the company to feel like a family, and this was a way to get everybody together under one roof and say we're all working together as a team, focused on the same objectives, and here to help each other. And to give them visions and inspiration for the future. It really worked. Where we got the most traction in these retreats was the socialization taking place, the informal at-dinner conversation, learning trade secrets from each other – just a great way to cross-pollinate."

Sometimes the pollination took bizarre forms. In Acapulco during the late '80s, Scott had a late-night call that three managers had been drinking on the beach, one went for a swim, and when he didn't return, the other two went in after him. The first fellow washed up on shore, water-logged but alive, but his would-be rescuers were missing. After hotel-security and military people warned Scott that the undertow had probably claimed them, he signed papers instructing authorities how to handle their bodies. "Then I called John and Tom and told them what had happened. About three or four hours later, as it was starting to get light, I was sitting with them talking in the lobby when all of a sudden these two guys walk in." Night fishermen had picked them up in their boats about a mile offshore. "That evening, at our banquet, one of the guys was joking about it and I just couldn't handle it any more. This is the only time that this has ever happened in my life, but because I had gone through so much thinking that they'd died, and signing papers, and wondering how to communicate with the family, I grabbed the guy and threw him down on the table and caused a pretty big scene."

That incident was a dramatic exception to the generally happy scenarios that sent managers and, later, supervisors back home from retreats with renewed enthusiasm for their work. Management considers these get-togethers so vital that when there was talk about ending them a decade ago, the consensus within the company was to continue them despite the expense. "It costs a lot of money," Tom says, "but it's a shrewd investment at the end of the day. People bond at the retreats. And, you know, it's a sneaky way to get them to learn a lot – and then they go back incredibly energized."

A third important pillar of the company's success – along with pleasing customers and employees – was making sure that the charitable partners handled the relations with their donors professionally. Wayne Penner had earned his wings working with non-profits in B.C., streamlining the telephone-solicitation offices, making them airier and more open, and being a benign boss to his solicitors: "On a four-hour shift, if we had our quota, I'd let them go after three hours. On a sunny day, we had phones with very long cords so they could work outside." In 1983 he was the first person associated with the company to use computers to generate phone-call lists. Two years later, Tom asked him to come on staff in the U.S. to help turn around stores with under-performing sources of supply.

Among them was a Spokane outlet supplied by a charity for the mentally handicapped. "It was in bad, bad shape – never did more than five hundred OKs a week. We fired the manager and I started to listen to how people were talking on the phone." Wayne told the solicitors: "You're not calling up people to ask for donations because the first thing they think is money. You're now an advertiser telling them that we'll have

a truck in their neighborhood – not 'area,' which sounds cold and calcu-
lated – and could we stop by their house to pick up things they no longer
need. We're not reminding them that we're picking up, we're *confirming*.
And remember that silence is golden, so as people are thinking, you jump
in very slowly to say we take pots and pans, toys, dishes, books, any kind
of clothing. And after you say all that, the homeowner knows she has
something for us."

As Wayne knew, the solicitors now felt better about themselves
by offering a service rather than begging for donations. The results were
heartening: "My mission was to reach a quota of eight hundred OKs a
week [up from five hundred] and the store would be a success. After a
month, we did exactly one thousand. We'd gone from terrible to fantastic."

PEDAL TO THE METAL

Mike Griffith has a fascinating explanation of how Savers grew across
North America: "We opened stores where Tom had vacations. Skiing in
Denver, he'd scope out other thrift stores. He'd spend a full day driving the city. The best example was Phoenix, which opened in 1988.
He'd gone there and come back with rental-car maps circled with realtors' offices. He went on vacation to Hawaii and said there were no thrift
stores there." Even when not holidaying, Tom was game to visit out-of-
the-way places. "None of us would ever have opened a store in Winnipeg.
Or flown to Saskatchewan." Tom agrees: "When I went to New England
with my family in 1993, I could see the opportunities, and within a year
we had stores there. Albuquerque was another one because I went skiing
in Taos, New Mexico, and thought, Wow, this is a great market – and it
has been."

Chris Barton, the Vancouver real-estate broker, has his own stories about Tom: "He looks at a property and says, 'I want to do this.' Not
a lot of analysis – a gut feel, seeing the street, the building, and the pulse
of the area. He has a phenomenal memory: He'll know every major street
in Canada in every city over 50,000 population – without a map. On
the Prairies we'd fly in and rent a car. Tom is a good driver and he's very
quick. If we went too far, he'd do an immediate U-turn in the middle of

the street." Tom remembers another time, in Montreal: "The speed limit was probably about sixty kilometres an hour and I just hit the brakes and pulled a U. Chris, in the back seat, could see a car coming at him so he was screaming while Rod was in the front, laughing."

Rod VanLeeuwen went on most of those trips and came to know Chris's expertise in finding possible store sites. "He'd throw them up and we'd shoot them down. Chris has been as close to the company as anybody who isn't on the payroll. He was involved in most of the Canadian real-estate selection – ninety-plus properties."

"We were the first of our kind of store in Canada," Tom reflects. "So we had a better hit ratio there: every single Canadian store we ever opened was at some level a winner. [However, three unprofitable stores have closed in the years since, in New Westminster, B.C., Chicoutimi, Quebec, and Whitehorse, Yukon.] We wanted to become a national retailer in Canada in a hurry and build a defensible competitive position before anybody else." In trading areas of at least 100,000 people, the trio scouted main streets for recycled buildings of at least 25,000 square feet with parking and loading facilities. Often the location had formerly housed a supermarket. "When food stores close a location," Chris says, "they don't want their competitors coming in there and so they kill the site by putting in a strong financial company like Value Village. We give them a restrictive-use clause, which is basically that we won't sell food or drugs."

Chris was a good road companion, with his relaxed manner (he may be the only realtor in North America who still doesn't own a cellphone). And the traveling wasn't all business, as he dramatizes in recounting a winter trip to Saskatchewan with Tom and Rod. After dinner, his companions decided to play some pranks on him. "They came in smoking cigars to make my room stink and turned the heat up to 100 degrees – and you couldn't open the window. They put in a four o'clock wake-up call for me and the next morning asked, 'How did you sleep?' And I said, 'The stupid front desk called me at four o'clock and the place was so hot.'"

Tom looks back with fondness on those days: "I was everywhere in Canada and the U.S. and making those trips with Rod or John or Chris was just a fun process. After Jeff left the company, I'd gone to Rod with a proposition: 'I will make you VP of the company, plus I will pay you a success fee, if you can execute a plan to open all of these stores by these dates in Canada.' Rod is my alter ego. He is a completely different thinker than I am. He's not quiet, but he is analytical while I'm a quick trigger-puller – to my own detriment at times. You tell me something and I've got a real opinion about it real quick. Tell him something and it will take him a day or two, but when he comes back to you he's thought it through completely and has a good game plan on how to execute it."

Or, as Mike Griffith puts it, "When Rod hooked up with Tom, they became a dynamite combo. He took Tom's go-go-go and coalesced it into an operations plan." After overseeing the Canadian stores all those years – across the breadth of the country from the Pacific west coast to the Atlantic Maritime provinces – Rod says, "I know Canada better than my own country, as far as the geography is concerned. We spent a lot of time driving these towns so when people presented opportunities, we'd *know* them."

SHANNON SHAKES THINGS UP

Once this roving selection trio found the right sites, it became Shannon Givens's job to get the new stores up and running. Her first encounter with Rod as Canadian VP in the late 1980s had been less than auspicious. He'd observed her and her team members on a sales day when she was manager of the largest Vancouver store, the Victoria Drive location. "We had a managers' meeting the next day," Shannon says, "and he shared with us what he thought of our management – and it was not very pretty. I remember sitting there and thinking, *Who the hell do you think you are, Mr. Rod VanLeeuwen? That is the last time I am going to hear that out of your mouth.* So the next sale day I pulled my team together and told them about the managers' meeting. We bought Value Village tee-shirts for the entire crew so they could all be identified on the floor. We broke the store into sections and made people accountable for each section. We set a standard together as a management team about what we thought the store needed to look like, and after we all agreed, I said, 'Okay I am holding everyone accountable for their jobs.' And the next time that Rod came in on the sale day, he leaned against a rack and said, 'I really like your tee-shirts; you can really identify them out on the floor. This is a big change from last time – what did you do?' And when I explained to him what we'd worked on, he was pretty impressed, and I didn't think he was quite the jerk I felt he was originally. He became a tremendous mentor for me."

Rod later asked Shannon to take over a struggling store in Calgary as a first step to becoming a district manager. Ray Duplessis, who'd been in charge of Alberta operations, was moving to Montreal to open the initial Quebec store. She found the Calgary outlet a mess, with an unresponsive staff and a Back Room piled high with too much merchandise and an adjoining 15,000-square-foot warehouse bursting with other goods. "The previous manager had been let go for fudging the numbers and he'd been storing merchandise back there."

Shannon fired the store's production supervisor, got ruthless about weeding out anything marginal from her stock, and shipped some of the overburden of product to stores in Edmonton. Within nine weeks she had the warehouse cleared. Then she herself swept it out and brought her team members to view the empty space. "You guys, see this floor? It stays like this – not one bag, not one box, *nothing* gets put back here. We need to pretend this room doesn't exist." When she returned from a few days off, there was a single box in the warehouse; it was empty, a friendly joke from her staff. The weekly sales of $25,000 soon doubled and later in the year reached an impressive $60,000.

Alberta proved eventful for the indefatigable Shannon, who soon became a district manager there, began a relationship, and gave birth to a son in 1991. The previous year, during her pregnancy, she was traveling from city to city as she helped launch five stores across western Canada: the first Villages in Saskatchewan, on her home turf of Saskatoon, and the provincial capital of Regina; second outlets in each of Winnipeg and Calgary; and a third one in Edmonton.

Her older brother, Dale Givens, was a manager in training in Calgary when she called on him to assist in the grand opening of the Winnipeg store. To keep people sane during the hurly-burly of preparation, she liked to play practical jokes. "I really had never played one on my brother. There was a girl named Sheila in our marketing department who'd attended many grand openings with me and I told her my brother would be up on the scaffolding helping her put the store graphics on the wall. 'And I just want to tell you, being his sister, that my brother sometimes oversteps his bounds. He will intentionally get close to you. His hand may casually drape over your shoulder or your butt. And you are well within your rights to smack him and tell him to back off.'

"Then I told my brother: 'Sheila went sky-diving and popped her ears, so you have to get close to her so she can hear you.' And Rod and I watched the two of them and were howling. Sheila would not walk in front of Dale – she always made sure there was some distance – and meanwhile he's trying to get close to her. That night Dale told me, 'I don't know what you are talking about, she hears just fine.' It was the next morning that we finally 'fessed up to what was happening and everybody cracked up and swore that they would get me." Dale went on to manage the original Calgary store and to become district manager for Alberta, Saskatchewan, and Manitoba.

The opening of the second outlet in Calgary, #219, was far less fun. It was a new mega-Village spread over more than 35,000 square feet. The contractor was so far behind in construction that on the first day the parking lot had no lights and pavers were still laying bricks inside the store. The staff, meanwhile, were mostly inexperienced. "Calgary was booming and it was really difficult to hire staff," Shannon says. "We were hiring bodies as they walked in. We were over-supplied on the miscel and had a ton of merchandise in the Back Room, so we had challenges there. We nicknamed the store '666' because there was not one area that went right." As it turned out, the store was a success from the start.

After all this, while fighting the flu and dealing with a manager stealing money from the store in Regina, Shannon managed to have her baby. Five weeks later, she was back at work with the help of a sister and a sister-in-law to care for her son. In 1992, with her relationship with his father ended, she asked Tom and Rod for a transfer back to Vancouver. Although she was willing to return as a store manager, they offered her the new position of Canadian general manager, working with the district managers of all twenty-six stores. Among them were two new ones in Ontario, the country's major population center. The first outlet in the province was in the southwestern city of London, the second in the city of Mississauga, adjoining Toronto – the metropolis the company had found too expensive four years before – where the stores tended to be in the inner city. Now a second Village was about to open in Mississauga. (Today, the Ontario market has forty-one outlets and is expected to grow beyond fifty.)

Mike Davison, then one of the district managers in western Canada, says, "Shannon really understood the business and knew that production was the heart of it. We were best friends. We used to go on retreats and we were the party animals." She'd first worked for Mike when he managed the Langley, B.C., store. He was always content to remain in Vancouver, "where I do my best work" – and where he earned the reputation of Hatchet Man for his propensity to fire managers who were failing to live up to his standards or, even worse, stealing from their stores.

At a company retreat, Mike was introduced to the principle of "managing by walking around" and embraced it heartily. "My most productive work was wandering through a store. I'd go into a store not as the DM [district manager]. When I pulled into the parking lot, I was looking at it from a customer perspective: Is it clean and organized? Are the signs straight? Is this a place that I would want to go into? Walking into the front door, I stopped and stood there: is there something in this place that wows me and draws me over to something of interest? If I spent half a day Monday and Friday in the office, the rest of the time I would be out in the stores talking to customers and employees. I wandered through the production room and said to a pricer, 'Hey, Sally, how's it going?' I would always do my homework and check the sales ahead of time. I'd know if she was in the top ten in Canada and say, 'Sally, I see you were sixth last week. Congratulations, good job' – and yell that in front of twenty people in the Back Room because they were going to want to do that too."

One of Mike's major contributions was his realization in the early '90s that the company could capitalize on customers' natural inclination to come to thrift stores to buy used clothing and other paraphernalia for Halloween. "I was talking to my store managers and everybody is just throwing in their ideas. I asked, How do we get more business in October than we already have? Why don't we sell new Halloween costumes?" He sourced two wholesalers in Seattle that offered such garb and masks and began selling them well before Halloween. Even though the profit margins were small, his stores made money on the products and the take kept increasing each year. The eventual target – which was hit – was for each outlet to sell $100,000 worth of new Halloween merchandise, purposely spread over several departments to lure the customer through a store. Mike even took to distributing an annual poem proclaiming the benefits of the Halloween push and mocking those managers who rebelled at it. An excerpt:

> *The managers were grumpy and scratchin' their heads:*
> *"We got no more room to display all the dead.*
> *Our racks are so full, we won't give up space.*
> *Used is our business, not 'New' in its place."*

Mike Davison's gut instinct about the possibilities of Halloween would later prove out as sales of costumes featuring phantoms and other frightening creatures exploded over the next decade and a half to make the season the highlight of the retail year.

These are the good ghosts and goblins in the company's chronicle. But there have been other, less-kindly bogeymen that have kept bedeviling Savers throughout its history.

"Within six minutes, the store was engulfed in flames."

CRITICS AND FRIENDS

CHAPTER SIX

From the tone of its headline and lead paragraphs, the story in the *Los Angeles Times* sounded like very bad news:

> *Donated Goods Form Heart of a Billion-Dollar Family Empire*
>
> In the beginning, the Ellisons salvaged troubled souls. Now they make fortunes in salvage.
>
> A mostly reclusive family of Salvation Army officers turned entrepreneurs, the Ellisons dominate a flourishing multibillion-dollar trade in used clothing and household items solicited in the name of charity and sold in thrift stores heralding the names of those charities.
>
> The family, their associates and former employees who have struck out on their own quietly run hundreds of such stores coast-to-coast and in Canada, unseen by the public or even most government officials charged with regulating charities.

The article, published in 1987, went on to say that the *Times* had investigated several thousand tax returns of American charities and conducted interviews with 100-plus thrift-store operators, not-for-profits' executives, and government officials. These had revealed that the opera-

Opposite: Employees became heroes in a fire that closed the Village in Langley, B.C.

tors got the lion's share of the proceeds from donated merchandise – sometimes making as much as $2.55 for each dollar a charity received for the use of its name to solicit goods from householders.

The report recounted how Ben and Orlo Ellison were Sally Ann officers who'd gone into business for themselves and how their brothers Robert, Walter, and John followed them into the thrift industry. "All five brothers are now dead, but today nearly 100 Ellisons, their in-laws, associates and former employees run hundreds of thrift stores in Los Angeles, Ventura, Seattle, Atlanta, Tampa, Denver, Chicago and other cities in almost every state."

The Times reporter quoted the general manager of the Los Angeles Social Service Department about one operator's relationship with a local charity: "What the California Council of the Blind is doing is selling their name for ten cents on the dollar. They don't control the store, they don't hire the solicitors, they just let [him] use their name."

One of the extended-family members interviewed was Ray Ellison, Orlo's son, operator of M & M Management Co. of Ventura, California, which then had charitable clients in seven states ("he declined to say just how many") and in one recent year supposedly charged a disabled veterans' organization $46,000 more than the charity spent on all its services. One vets' store allegedly paid Ray's brother, Robert, more than $81,000 for part-time work while Ray's son Matthew generated $1.3-million from charity-linked thrift stores in less than six years. There was a quote from Ben Ellison, a grandson of John Ellison (the original Ben's brother), who was a part-owner of a thrift-shop chain in Chicago: "The reason we are successful is that we know how to take junk and merchandise it."

For Bill Ellison and his sons in Bellevue, none of the insinuations was surprising.

Plowing through the 5,500-word story, they had to wonder whether they would be tarred with the brush of taking advantage of the not-for-profits' "junk" and turning it into treasure for the prime benefit of their family business.

But in fact the reporter focused mostly on employees who'd worked for Ellisons across the country and were now operating on their own. For example, the fellow in California whose business arrangement apparently gave a council for the blind only ten per cent of a store's gross revenues.

Or the two ex-employees of John Ellison, who were now based in Florida and ran ten stores for a charity in Illinois, earning more than 100-per-cent annual return on their equity. The article, in dealing with Ray Ellison's M & M Management, treaded more carefully, reporting that a couple of the charities involved spoke favorably of their relationship with him ("This is the best deal we can find") – although one veterans' group had bought out their contract with M & M and was now making as much as thirty-six-per-cent profit on sales.

And when the story did get around to the Ellisons of Bellevue, it was remarkably fair. Tom was first quoted about being at a 1984 reunion of about 150 members of the extended family at his Uncle John's home in Sequim, Washington: "I wanted to ask my cousins about the business, but everyone is so secretive about how they operate that no one discussed it."

Later the reporter contrasted the Bellevue-based operations with others in the business:

> Several charity regulators said that the best deal for charities that choose to contract with a for-profit company is a wholesale buy-sell agreement. All cited TVI, Inc., of Bellevue, Wash., as a model.
>
> "We put up the cash, we assume all the liability," said Tom Ellison, vice-president of the firm, which public records indicate has annual sales of $25 million. In southern California TVI operates one store, in Buena Park, which buys, wholesale, items donated to the Children's Home Society in Los Angeles.
>
> "Basically, there are two sides to this business – soliciting and selling. The way we do it, the drivers and callers work for the charity, which sends us a bill for their pay each month and we reimburse them," Tom Ellison said.
>
> "We then buy the goods wholesale and sell them in our stores, which have names like Thrift Village. We don't use the name of the charity in the store. We want to be like Kinney Shoes. They buy goods from wholesalers and unless

there is a brand name you don't know who the wholesaler is," Tom Ellison added.

In addition, TVI splits each store's operating profit with the charity 50-50. Tom Ellison said that TVI's 6 per cent to 7 per cent in management costs come out of its half of the profits.

"We could make a lot more than we do, do what some of my relatives do," said Tom Ellison's father, TVI President William O. Ellison. "But I long ago decided I would rather have a sound business that would prosper and grow and do a lot of good than make every buck I could.

"I am in favor of sound, intelligent regulation of the business," he added.

GOOD WILL AND BAD

Over the next decade, the company – operating as TVI and later as Savers – would receive more journalistic bouquets along with several brickbats that attacked its entrepreneurial approach to doing business in the U.S. and Canada.

In 1991 the *Calgary Herald* reported complaints from both house-holders and not-for-profit organizations about the presence of two Value Villages in the city. The operator of one charity shop charged that the for-profit Villages – by collecting merchandise for a local mentally handi-capped group using "aggressive, slick telephone soliciting" – were drying up the supply of used goods for her operation. A second article, headlined "Thrift store owners live in lap of luxury," pointed out that Bill Ellison was an American who owned an expensive house on Lake Washington.

It didn't take long for counter-arguments to appear in the newspa-per. Bill Lockhart, executive director of the Alberta Institute on Mental Retardation, wrote in a long, published letter to the editor that the Elli-sons were "a very reputable family." Their partnering style, he noted, "has opened the door for a number of charities and non-profit groups to rely less on begging for cash and government handouts and more on self-initiative in a much-needed environmenally sound business of recycling furniture and clothing no longer of use.... Rather than criticizing this spirit of entrepreneurship and creative partnership, we should be applauding the effort." He said that in the past year, thanks to the relationship with the Villages, the Alberta Association for Community Living had more than $780,000 available for its cause. And his own institute was able to provide meaningful jobs for seventy-two mentally handicapped people.

Another letter-writer observed that the deal between the charity and the Villages "is no different in principle from what the Boy Scouts do when they sell bottles from a bottle drive to a profit-making bottle depot."

A more pointed assault on the company came several years later from *Alberta Report*, a now-defunct conservative magazine. This time the article was titled "'Charity' for billionaires" and it was rife with errors. Citing the *Los Angeles Times* exposé, it lumped the owners of the local Value Villages with the Ellisons of the extended family and their former employees – without mentioning that the newspaper had presented Bill Ellison and his sons as model operators. A photograph of an Association for Community Living truck carried the blatantly false caption: "Almost none of the proceeds go to the disabled." A year later a sister publication, *Western Report*, was a bit more balanced: while claiming that the Villages had "grabbed a near-monopoly on used goods," it admitted that the relationship between the company and its charities was profitable for both parties. It also quoted an executive director of the Cerebral Palsy Association, a second Alberta charity working with the company: "The contract with Value Village has breathed new life into this organization." (The Ontario Cerebral Palsy Foundation later made a similar spirited defence of its Village liaison in a *Canadian Business* magazine article – remarking on the spinoff jobs being created and the nearly $800,000 the deal had provided the organization the previous year.)

It's not only Canadian media and not-for-profit charities that have set their gunsights on Savers. In 1992 four charities, including the Salvation Army, ran an ad welcoming one of the company's new thrift department stores to Sparks, Nevada – along with a chauvinistic invitation to shoppers to visit their outlets too ("you are helping local people help themselves"). Then the *Reno Gazette-Journal* quoted officials of one of the charities publicly deploring the presence of a for-profit competitor. As the newspaper commented, "The concern is that merchandise that normally might go to a non-profit agency to employ, clothe and feed the community's needy or pay for service programs now creates profits for an out-of-state company." But it did allow a response from Scott Blomquist, who by then was Savers' human-resources director: "Over the last five years we've been expanding into new markets and invariably local thrift operators and charities get somewhat paranoid that donations will dry up." In fact, he said, the donations to not-for-profits increase because of the heightened community awareness about thrift stores.

Of all the charitable organizations, Goodwill Industries has always seen Savers (and TVI before it) as a major competitor in a rivalry that reached a peak in the '90s – when Goodwill's director of brand management issued a memo to the CEOs of its autonomous member groups. In a backhanded way, it was a flattering portrait of the company: "For-profit stores and chains continue to pose a threat to Goodwill Industries retail operations, particularly those owned and operated by the Ellison family and TVI.... We have historically benchmarked our successes by measuring our collections against each other, or against the equally comfortable Salvation Army and other, smaller not-for-profit organizations. But new market entrants, mostly for-profits, have demonstrated through innovative practices that the overall donated-goods market is much larger. Capturing this market, however, may cost more per pound collected and require collection techniques that are perhaps best termed 'aggressive convenience.' That is, working harder to offer more convenient donation locations and times, and otherwise making it easy for not single, but repeated, donations to occur."

That memo telegraphed just how intensely some Goodwill Industries operators felt about Savers. At the time, however, the for-profit company was generally unconcerned about its not-for-profit competition – as Tom Ellison admits: "We didn't pay any attention to Goodwill through the '70s or '80s because they just weren't a blip on our radar screen. They had a lot of stores, but they were always dark and dingy and they just didn't matter to us. And shame on us, because we were really asleep at the wheel when Michael Miller took charge of Goodwill in Portland, Oregon, and began to turn things around.

"But if you think how easy it would be, with a little bit of know-how, to do that when you have no cost of goods and your payroll is your only program expense. And their customers don't have to pay sales tax and Goodwill doesn't have to pay income tax. They have a tremendous brand and they get free merchandise – so they have a thirty-per-cent margin over us, which is unheard of. Wal-Mart may have a one- or two-percent margin over Target or K-Mart. Goodwill has a minimum thirty-percent advantage over us, so a Goodwill store should be able to clean our clocks. In most cases, they still don't, but they can, and so we have to be on top of our game. When you get Goodwills in Portland or other parts of the country that are really starting to wake up and do it right, they become cash machines.

"The Portland operation is such a cash machine that they're looking for ways to spend the money. They have built a huge facility, which handles advertising for Goodwills all over the country – but they sell it, they don't give it away. And they have loaned money, as far as we know, to Goodwills in Honolulu and to Edmonton to try to hurt us. Their mission really is to take us down if they can. They say that we may know the retail business very well, but we don't have the one brand across North America that they have and they can exploit that if they over-collect merchandise and take it away from us and our suppliers. And then they go around and describe us as the evil empire."

In late 2004 news media in Oregon announced that Michael Miller, who runs the Goodwill stores in Portland and the Columbia Willamette region, had earned more than $785,000 in annual compensation the previous year. The reports prompted a backlash among donors throughout the state. For example, the Southern Oregon Goodwill Industries operation – which had just distributed thousands of direct mailings for a holiday fund drive – was fielding responses from potential donors who were refusing to donate any goods to the charity. As the local Goodwill president reported, "People who saw the article are responding right away, in the negative. Some of them quote the article themselves, and others just send back the entire newspaper clipping."

LABOR PAINS

Beyond the skeptical media and those charities that considered Savers as a serious rival, if not an outright enemy, there were other outsiders who challenged the company's business style. Over the years, some unions have viewed the employees of this successful chain of thrift department stores as a tempting target to organize. Much more so in Canada, where labor groups seem more deeply entrenched than in the U.S.

In the late '80s a couple of different unions approached staff at two B.C. Villages. Nineteen employees at the New Westminster location in Greater Vancouver decided to join the General Workers Union in 1988 and began trying to negotiate a first contract with the company. When a provincial mediator failed to resolve the dispute over wages, the union went on strike two months later. Organizers hoped to sign up team members in all the stores in the province, but those at a nearby outlet in Coquitlam were quickly quoted in the local media as saying they had no grievances with management.

Meanwhile, a local of the Teamsters Union organized employees at the Langley store and when negotiations broke down in June '89, the Village was closed for the summer. After a new management offer in September, which the union refused, picketers were no longer officially locked out but on strike. The store reopened in September with managers and then replacement workers, but because the local charity wouldn't cross picket lines, it was stocked with merchandise from an Alberta charity.

District manager Mike Davison, who'd once run the Langley store, remembers receiving two phone calls on the same day. "We've got the General Workers on an organizing drive in our New West store and then I get a call that the Teamsters are banging on the door at our Langley store. So I'm scrambling. Because I was most concerned about the Teamsters, I go flying out to Langley and there are union leaflets all over the lunchroom table. Nancy Bryce, a fairly new store manager, was packed and gone within two days once the union came – she was transferred out to a Value Village in Winnipeg [because of her relative inexperience]. My next manager-in-training was Brian Avery and I said, 'Brian, we have got a big challenge in this store.' The union certification was a done deal as far as I

The Alberta Association for Community Living helps children have good community access – as Carmen (in a wheelchair) has on this Girl Guide field trip with friends.

could see. We had a great team of people there that were bamboozled into joining the union, and they were playing all kind of weird games."

Tom Ellison and Rod VanLeeuwen hired a team of lawyers from Laing Brown's firm as well as a consultant to help Mike negotiate with the Teamsters. "We were meeting at a hotel in Langley with this consultant who was supposed to be working on my behalf," Mike says. "We wanted to make it clean and simple – easy for us to continue running our business – but the Teamsters would have no part of that. And the consultant was taking me outside all the time, telling me that I'm being a stubborn sonuvabitch and I'm going to have to live with the deal sooner or later and so why not accept some of the contract language? I said I couldn't – it would strangle how we did business. Finally, I just told him he was fired and then I called Rod and said I wanted to do it on my own with one of the lawyers. But when we couldn't do a deal, we just turned the lights out and shut the door with all the picket lines out front – and went home. A few months later, at a supervisors' retreat, Tom [who owned the store site] said he thought it was time that we opened up Langley again and I said I'd give it a shot."

After Brian Avery hired new staff, he and Mike had to resort to a cloak-and-dagger approach in supplying the Langley location. Mike: "We were pulling merchandise across the country – by Teamsters, no less, but they couldn't deliver right to the store so they would drop it [somewhere else]. Then we hired a friend of mine to do midnight runs. We had walk-ie-talkies because there were picketers around the store, sleeping in their cars. We rented a tractor-trailer, made sure that someone was there with the gates open, and zoomed in and closed the gates. Although we didn't make as much money as the store could, we had it open."

The strike dragged on for seventeen months. "Finally we wanted the picket line gone and most of the employees had to find other jobs, which was was the unfortunate part of it. Gene Wirch, the head of the local, came to me and said, 'We need to talk.'

"I'd spoken to our lawyers and I told him, 'You are never going to win this; it's going to go on forever. What do you need?'

"And he said, 'If you write us a check' – and I think it was for $50,000 – 'we'll go away, we'll drop the certification.'

"'I'll tell you what: I will write out checks totalling $50,000 for the employees who are still walking the picket line, but I will not write any out for the Teamsters Union.' He paused for a while and we finally agreed to a gag order [to not make the deal public] – but the next day it hit the headlines of the newspaper: 'Teamsters sell out under pressure from Value Village.' But they were gone and it was great."

At the New Westminster store, the General Workers Union had successfully organized the employees but rejected a wage package Value Village was offering – sending their new members out on strike. It was at this point that a fresh face in the Canadian branch of the company sur-faced to help deal with the ensuing confrontation. Jeff Smail, twenty-eight at the time, had leased and run a western chain's service station at age seventeen (so young, his mother had to sign the leasing papers), which was soon in the chain's top ten for fuel sales. Later he managed U-Haul stores for seven years and sold life insurance before answering a blind ad for a management trainee for "a junior department store." It turned out to be Value Village, which his wife had discovered just a week before when she bought a pair of pants there for sixty-nine cents. When Jeff followed up on the ad and spotted thirty used crocheted or plastic Kleenex-box covers in the Hastings store, he wondered, *What am I doing here?*

But Mike Davison reassured him about the strength of the thrift-store industry and Jeff started as a trainee in January '89 – just in time to get involved in the New Westminster strike, which began on a sale day. "Mike needed people in a panic so four management trainees [MTs] ran cash registers with the store manager and stayed there for the duration of the strike. Out on the sidewalk the pickets were calling us names. The other MTs would lose it at times and I was often the one who would step in between." When a striker tossed a snowball that just missed his head, an unaware Jeff didn't flinch and earned a small reputation for his nerve. Inside the store, over about six weeks he tried to run the production room with five others. In a twelve-hour day he'd manage only twenty OKs "and butcher the pricing."

When picket-line actions threatened to reach the point of violence – strikers were swearing at customers – management decided to close the store. It reopened after only three days, with the twenty or so employees accepting a wage package they'd initially rejected. But the General Workers Union was soon swallowed up by the much-more-militant B.C. Government Employees Union. Management wanted the new union to extend the existing labor contract for a year. As Mike Davison relates, "the BCGEU were very intimidating around the bargaining table. We just shut the store down eventually" – because it proved unprofitable.

Another newcomer to the company got involved in the New Westminster store closure. Brenda Seraphim, born and raised in Toronto, had taken her final high-school years in Vancouver before studying international relations at the University of British Columbia. Seduced by the real world, she left to work for a personnel agency and a credit union and briefly was even a night-club cocktail waitress before finding her niche in the human-resources field. After five years in the personnel department of the Hotel Vancouver, she became a regional HR director for Delta Hotels – while volunteering heavily for Expo 86, Vancouver's World Exposition – and then an assistant HR director for the local Four Seasons hotel. Other stints followed, with a bottled-water company and a chopstick manufacturer and part-time teaching at a community college, until she landed a contract with Price Waterhouse to help shape a tourism-training program. And it just happened that the accounting and consulting firm was head-hunting for an HR manager for a company called Value Village Stores in Canada

Brenda veered between taking an HR position with CN, the major Canadian railway, and the one with this thrift-store chain she'd never heard of, which had twenty-six stores in Canada and overall sales of $47 million. When the thirty-year-old did decide to join the company in 1992, one of her first tasks was to handle the human factor in the closing and subsequent reopening of the New Westminster outlet.

She felt for the employees losing their jobs. With so few of them paying union dues, she says, "it was a money-losing situation for the BCGEU and they basically turned their backs on them. The union did nothing. We couldn't put them into another store because we didn't want another union. I asked Tom, 'Do you want to do the right thing for these people?' And he let me do it. I gave classes on how to write a resumé, wrote resumés for these people, prepared them for job interviews, and taught them how to present themselves."

Both Brenda Seraphim and Jeff Smail went on to become key characters in the Savers story under Shannon Givens's energetic leadership. And although Brenda hadn't been involved in the long strike at the Langley Village, she did witness another dramatic event that closed the store several years later.

At about six P.M. on May 21, 2002, a male customer told a cashier that he'd smelled something burning. Sales clerk Susie Lumanlan was checking the heaters in the restrooms upstairs when she noticed a customer go into the women's washroom. Susie, after using the staff washroom, emerged to hear an employee announcing a fire over the public-address system. Billowing smoke and flames filled the stairs leading down to the sales floor. Rather than leave immediately, Susie banged on the women's-washroom door to alert the customer – and to lead her to safety through a staff exit, which had to be opened with a coded lock. Meanwhile, the other four employees had quickly herded every shopper outside.

Brenda was there to watch the destruction and was one of the last to leave that night: "Within six minutes, the store was engulfed in flames. Though it was Seniors' Day, thank God the fire started (or was started) when most people were at home eating dinner, and no one was injured." But three firefighters suffered minor burns in a backdraft as they and nearly a hundred others from six different fire halls took two and a half hours to quell the blaze. The Langley department later awarded the quick-thinking Village employees plaques commending their bravery and the city council also praised them officially.

The store, which had about $5 million in damage, was closed and a new, larger one opened less than a year later – with the mother and son who were last to escape the burning Village becoming the first customers to walk into its successor.

Savers has managed to weather all these external forces of union organizers, fire, and the brimstone vitriol of its thrift-industry rivals. But through the later years of the 1990s, internal tensions were welling up within the company. They would transform it from a tight family business into a different kind of enterprise that would lead to turmoil at the top.

GOOD TIMES, TOUGH TIMES

CHAPTER SEVEN

Before the business began to stutter and stall like an overheated, under-fuelled car engine, there were many positive developments that accelerated the course of the company throughout the 1990s. New people with new ideas and a passion for growth helped propel Savers into new markets and a doubling of its retail stores. Among the newcomers early in the decade were Buddy Grimmett, Eric Farley, and Becky (Baxter) Henchman, all of whom were beginning long careers with Savers.

Buddy Grimmett is an air-force sergeant's son born in Louisiana and schooled in San Jose, California. That's where he played Triple A football and apprenticed as a carpenter before working as a loss-prevention and security officer for several discount stores, including K-Mart. In 1988 he moved to Seattle as district security manager for the discount chain Best Products. Although he may look like a big, bearded, bullet-headed biker, Buddy brought a certain sensitivity to his trade: after he caught a jewelry saleswoman stealing stock, she wrote him from jail that he was the nicest man she'd ever dealt with and apologized for causing him trouble.

Buddy joined Savers in 1991 as its first director of loss prevention. He realized quickly that this was a private family enterprise, not a traditional, publicly accountable retail business. Still, that didn't stop him from confronting Bill Ellison one day in a Value Village that was about to be launched in Kent, Washington. Bill (whom Buddy had already met) was wandering through the store when he picked up a gold-plated business-card case and put it in his pocket. "Excuse me," Buddy said, re-introduc-

Opposite: Customers and staff were divided over this cheeky ad campaign.

Eric Farley joined the company in 1991 as a promotions coordinator and eventually became director of a brand-building marketing department.

ing himself to the co-owner of the company, "you've just put something in your pocket. One of the reasons I was hired here was to set an example. I can't let you have that today. I can take it upstairs and put a note on the case to hold it for the opening."

Bill agreed, but Buddy thought later, *That's the dumbest thing I've ever done.* He immediately drove back to the corporate office and confessed to Tom what he'd said to his father. Tom laughed, but Buddy went home that night and told his wife he was going to get fired. The next day, Tom told him: "My dad thought it was funny. You've earned a lot of respect."

At a managers' retreat in Maui soon after, Buddy gave a workshop in which he described the new measures being taken to catch shoplifters – including alarms. And then he announced: "There are those of you who are either currently stealing or have stolen in the past. This is Amnesty Day. If any of you have caused any loss, that's water under the bridge. But moving forward, we have zero tolerance." Bill stood up and said, "I support this."

Yet over the following few months, Buddy did find several managers – some of them long-time employees – stealing money or merchandise from the company. They were all fired. Emboldened, he developed his department during the next three years, hiring seven people as district and regional managers to implement controls and educate the staff.

The same year Buddy was hired, Eric Farley came to Savers as a promotions coordinator to work with an advertising manager named Patty McShane. With a background in graphics and radio copywriting, Eric was soon immersed in creating promotional materials for special sales days at a Utah store and the grand opening of the Albuquerque store. He realized that there was a philosophical divide among the senior managers on the value of marketing to the company's archetypical customers, nicknamed Sue and Sam.

"Tom has a great sentiment about the company: if we build it and execute things correctly, we'll be successful. I tend to believe that's true. However, with our fast growth we've put stores in locations that are not optimal (and closed some of them) and we have to contend with outside influences like competition and shopping behavior and trends. At times, thrift stores are hot – the grungy '90s were pretty good for us. But there's always a role for telling our story: who we are and what we do. Scott Blomquist was a huge evangelist for marketing. He brought television advertising to the company.

"I happened to be the department manager for two of the most infamous sales-day spots produced. We still didn't have a lot of budget, so Scott said, 'Whatever we do, it needs to have an impact. We really need to go out there.' We called it the Full Moon Sale. In the print ad there was a guy with his crack showing above his jeans and the lines 'Half off all pants. 50% off everything else. Don't get left behind! Doors open at the crack of dawn.' Then we produced a TV commercial with a plumber making a house call who looks under the sink and there's a close-up of a real flesh-and-blood butt crack. The goal was to get noticed – and it was the best sales day we'd ever had. But we got a lot of phone calls protesting."

The ads – one of several informal, even silly campaigns – had been a surprise to many of the company's employees and may have marked a turning point in advertising philosophy. As Eric wrote in a memo to the stores, "Our revolutionary 'Full Moon Sale' seemed to split Team Members, Managers and Customers right down the middle. On one side were those that liked our cheeky (impudent; bold and shameless) humor designed to get attention, be memorable, and create word-of-mouth. On

Becky Henchman started as an events coordinator and later left the company – only to return as senior marketing and communications manager.

the other were those that felt we played to the lowest common denominator and crossed the line between base humor and bad taste. We can't argue with either camp. In the end, there was a lot of talk, and from the calls and letters that Marketing fielded, high-fivin' support and indignant moral outrage ran just about even. Are we going to do another 'Buttcrack Sale' anytime soon? Probably not. Was it worth doing? Probably so." Compared to the record February sale week the previous year, the current campaign was seven per cent higher in the U.S. and fifteen per cent in Canada. But John Bacon eventually declared that Savers was rebranding itself in a slightly more sophisticated way. "We could still be fun," Eric says, "but the idea was to create a brand that our team members and our customers feel comfortable with." Later, however, there would be other quirky campaigns, most centered on Halloween, but one back-to-school commercial that drew complaints showed a blonde teenager lusting after Value Village outfits and wise-cracking, "My mom says, 'At least she's never covered in tattoos.' And I say, 'What they don't know won't hurt them.'"

Becky Henchman (then Baxter) arrived as a twenty-seven-year-old in the department about six months after Eric. A journalism major in junior college, she'd graduated to work in marketing for a safety- and fire-products company in her hometown of Longview, Washington, before moving to Seattle. Answering an ad for a grand-opening coordinator for national ad campaigns, Becky learned that the employer was Savers. Never having been in a Value Village store, she visited one in nearby Lake City, which was then a shockingly shabby location done in the traditional brown tones. But the people at corporate office seemed professional and she took the job after a series of the company's typically intensive interviews.

On her first day on the job, she attended a President's Day sale at the Redmond store. "I was blown away. Not only did we struggle to find parking, but the people's carts were just mounded – they were spending so much money. It was a whole subculture/industry that I was never aware of." Within two months she helped open a store across the border in Burnaby, B.C. On the drive up to the Greater Vancouver area, Patty McShane's car broke down and they had to hitchhike with a Mormon family who took them to the border town of Blaine; Becky and Patty didn't arrive till the next afternoon. There she met the relaxed, wisecracking Mike Davison and saw a much prettier store, all spiffed up in teal-and-magenta hues.

As events coordinator she was responsible for identifying the advertising strategy, preparing an event budget, issuing press releases, coordinating entertainment, and getting the marketing materials to a store. "The ad strategy then was: 'How many sales are we going to have?' It's still not a company that culturally embraces marketing and advertising," she says, agreeing with Eric. "Tom and Rod believe that you don't need that much in the thrift industry."

When Patty left her post as ad manager, Becky co-managed the department with Eric until she began focusing on communications, management retreats, and special projects such as rebranding the stores. But the lack of emphasis on marketing and advertising finally frustrated her and Becky moved into sourcing – finding alternative supplies of merchandise beyond the company's existing charity partners. Finally she quit to work for a dot-com firm for two years, only to have Eric eventually lure her back to Savers.

MARCHING ACROSS CANADA

Throughout the early 1990s, the Canadian operation, with little direct competition, was expanding rapidly. But it wasn't necessarily contributing to the company's overall profit picture. "For the longest time," Tom says, "the U.S. was carrying Canada. As a company we were not making money up there. We had to invest and invest and invest. As we opened individual stores, they generally did make money right away, but we were investing so much that it took a long time to really start to turn the tide. I can remember from '90 to '92, at the peak of our growth in Canada – one year up there we grew eighty per cent – people in the company were asking, 'Why would you put this much capital into Canada? The corporation is not making any money.' Well, because we could see the potential."

That potential came to be realized over the next few years when Shannon Givens began collaborating more closely with Brenda Seraphim, directing the Canadian human-resources (HR) department, and Buddy Grimmett, running the overall Loss Prevention (LP) program. "What I was seeing in the field," Shannon says, "was that anytime there were questions about promotions or terminations or making management changes, they would always bubble up to me. I thought that the more we could push decision-making down the line, only the critical ones would come to me. I kept running into struggles with HR and LP and at one time the three of us were constantly butting our heads together. Then I started having a monthly meeting with Brenda and Buddy where we would talk about the stores and the needs, the policies and procedure standards. And we aligned ourselves and developed a comfort level to loosen up control."

"After stepping on each other's toes," Brenda continues, "we finally agreed upon our respective spans of control, including areas where they overlapped. We agreed to trust and rely on each other's area of expertise – operational, people, and protection of company assets. We were collaborative and inclusive in every sense of the words. If all three of us were aligned, we knew we were heading in the right direction. We then focused on pushing the decisions down and developing our direct reports – the people who reported directly to us. District managers, regional HR managers, and regional loss-prevention managers used the same three-pronged approach for managing the business in their geographic areas.

*Buddy Grimmett and
Brenda Seraphim at a 1992
supervisors' meeting.*

Our mandate to our direct reports was that if one of the three managers didn't agree with the direction being taken, that person was to consult with their boss and we would be the final decision-makers."

Eventually, Shannon says, "one of the biggest differences between Canada and the U.S. was that when problems would bubble up, my district managers would address them right away – and they had the authority to address them."

Before Brenda arrived, there hadn't been any consistent recruitment process. Adapting techniques from the tourism and hospitality industry to fit the retail trade, her human-resources department partnered with the operations people to find, hire, and then orient new employees – supplying the tools to find the best people and then working on-site to integrate them with management. Collaborating with district managers and loss-prevention managers, the HR team (including Marietta Ellen Macdonald, Ian Forrester, and Francine Farmer) conducted in-store meetings with hourly employees and managers in every store, asking both groups how they were being treated and what needed to improve.

Jeff Smail was typical of the managers who thrived in the process. In Langley, B.C., he had observed the way truck drivers unloaded their OKs – their bags of merchandise – onto store carts. The company was paying the charities on a per-cart basis and if there were fewer bags per cart, it was costing Savers money. Sometimes there'd be only twenty-four OKs instead of forty. What if we stack the bags like bricks? he wondered aloud. "One layer flat, the next standing on end, overlapping them to make a solid base. So we're not paying a hundred per cent for eighty per cent of the product. I used to drive people nuts making sure they knew how to stack carts properly." The technique eventually became enshrined as one of the corporate best practices.

In 1990 Jeff moved with his wife and ten-day-old son from B.C. to help open a store in Saskatoon, Saskatchewan. After Shannon sent him to a course called Management Action Planning in Calgary, he learned that he was a workaholic who was spreading himself too thinly. "Managing my time, I went from working twelve- to sixteen-hour days to where I could do all my work in eight hours and spend a lot of time walking the floor, getting team members to think about the business instead of being told what to do all the time." The store became so efficient that he became bored and welcomed a transfer as a district manager in Winnipeg and northwestern Ontario before taking on the DM's role for several stores in that province's densely populated southwestern region.

Over the decade, the Canadians' efficiency and inclusive approach combined to increase the business to ninety-two stores from twenty-six – with thirty-four of them in Ontario, where the company had enjoyed no brand recognition compared to western Canada and the U.S. Rod VanLeeuwen was forever roaming the nation to check out potential new store sites. "I always joked with him that there'd been Rod sightings – wherever he was looking for real estate," Brenda says. "Somebody would phone me and say, 'I've seen Rod. He's north of Saskatoon.' And as long as we hit our financial targets and took care of charities and people, Rod and Tom empowered us to get the job done with very little redirection from them. We were given clear goals, unlimited opportunity, and the freedom to operate separately from the American side of the business." Among other achievements, the team reduced the time it took to open a new store from as many as twelve weeks down to four – and ninety per cent of new Canadian stores were profitable in less than a year.

This collective success across Canada was driven by the ever-increasing involvement of the Canadian Diabetes Association (CDA). Tom describes the birth of the company's relationship with the charity: "It was around the time that we opened our first store in Edmonton. We had seven stores total in Canada and had never had two suppliers in the same town – and it makes sense to have multiple suppliers in an area. I could see that we were going to open up more stores in Vancouver and the Vancouver-Richmond Association could not possibly meet the demand. So I called our real-estate consultant in Vancouver, Chris Barton, who was working with the Royal LePage real-estate firm. Chris said, 'Peter Maddocks, who runs our office, is on the provincial board of the Canadian Diabetes Association; let me ask them if they have any interest.' I had a call from Peter within forty-eight hours saying they were interested. It was completely new to them. In those days it wasn't so centralized – B.C. did what they wanted."

The relationship clicked immediately and the local association began making so much money that in 1989, when Tom approached the Manitoba branch in Winnipeg, the director was keen to sign a similar agreement. "Then we went with CDA in Ontario and that's where the spark really lit the big fire." The insightful Jim O'Brien was running the Toronto office of Canadian Diabetes – then a loose collective of independently run provincial organizations sprinkled across the nation – and it was he who foresaw the tremendous potential of partnering with Savers. "They slowly began to make it into a truly national organization," Tom says today, "and now with their pickup program in almost every major city, Canadian Diabetes is sort of the Goodwill of Canada." (The CDA recognized the relationship not long ago with an award to Savers that "pays tribute to ongoing collaboration and teamwork to achieve common goals, making a difference in the lives of those living with diabetes." And Tom says it all started with Peter Maddocks, who has two daughters with the disease.)

A key factor in this growth was the work of Glenn Manderson, the charity's vice-president and national director of business operations. He joined the organization in 1996 after a career that included five years with the Canadian Red Cross as director of blood-donor recruitment. Seeing the potential of a closer involvement with the retail chain, he suggested to Jim O'Brien that Canadian Diabetes become more proactive. He approached Ray Bryce, who had once worked for CDA and was now Savers' Canadian director of vendor relations – the liaison with the charities supplying merchandise to the company. Two new Value Villages were being planned for Ontario and one in Newfoundland. Glenn suggested that his charity could supply them all with donations. When Ray reacted negatively, Glenn and Jim went to Bellevue to pitch Tom and Rod directly. As Glenn recalls the meeting, "Jim described how his vision was to be one of the leading diabetes organizations in the world and to do this we needed to grow from a $43-million-dollar-a-year business to a $100-million one. And I said I [the business-operations department] needed to be $30 million of that. You could have heard a pin drop." At the time, CDA was supplying Savers with only $8 million worth of goods.

While they didn't get to be the supplier for one of the Ontario stores, Savers did meet with them again not long after. Would they take on the second location in that province as well as the outlet in Newfoundland because the original charity partners were fumbling badly? Then there were other stores in Ontario and Alberta – and would CDA partner there too? "They said they wanted to grow and wanted us to be a key component of that," Glenn recounts. "I came out of that meeting flying. The next two years of my life, it was ninety-hour work weeks. I was gone twenty-six weekends a year. In one year we added fourteen new operations alone."

Glenn Manderson's business-operations revenue has now hit that dreamed-of $30 million, most of it derived from the affiliation with Savers, which receives just under half of its Canadian merchandise from CDA.

TRAINING IN AMERICA

The American stores, meanwhile, were on their own growth curve – slower but steady. In the five years after the successful launch of the new-look Phoenix store in 1988, John Bacon was spearheading the planning and design of two more outlets in the state capital and one in Mesa, Arizona. And he and his team were opening locations not only in the Pacific Northwest states of Oregon and Washington but also in Alaska and Hawaii and into the Midwest as well as the West: Minnesota, New Mexico, Nevada, Texas, Idaho, and Utah.

One of the new stores was based in Orem, amid northcentral Utah's

Rocky Mountains, and it was there that Savers decided to locate its first training center. With the explosion of outlets, the company needed an on-going supply of store managers to run them and district managers to oversee operations. By now Scott Blomquist had created a department of human resources and in 1992 was named director of HR. Early on, he says, Bill Ellison had encouraged a loose form of management training, clearing space in the warehouse in Renton, Washington, and bringing trainees in to hear tapes by motivational speakers such as Zig Ziglar and Wayne Dyer. These sessions evolved into the managers' and supervisors' retreats and then, in 1991, a dedicated training center in Orem.

John Booth, a training and development manager, had set up the program to train employees from both the U.S. and Canada as production and operation supervisors and store managers. Over eleven to fourteen weeks more than fifty people at times lived at Brigham Young University while getting some theory and hands-on experience in the local store, everything from sales to administration. They would then be sent across the continent to work in those areas that needed them. Celeste Vanecko, an experienced educator, worked with John and then succeeded him.

Not long after joining Savers in 1992, Brenda Seraphim flew down to Orem to study the program. She had a mixed reaction to the training center: "It was like adult camp. I was stapling and racking in the store and then went back to the university at 4 P.M. (It was the first time in my adult life that I didn't bring my work home with me.) I had a great six weeks. But at that time, the training was all done by rote. They spent a lot of time on task-oriented things versus teaching people how to lead. I was asked to go there to look at how people can learn the business and also to set up a training center in Canada because it was getting progressively more difficult to get Canadians to go down there. I came back to Canada wanting to focus a bit more on the management side of things. We opened a training center in Cambridge, Ontario, hired a training manager – and then closed it down a few months later for financial reasons."

Shannon Givens explains: "The concept of a training center is good. The reality is that there's a lot of hardship: you're asking people to go live somewhere for several weeks to go through a training program. And it's very hard for people to understand Value Village unless they're in the company and can see it and feel it and be in the store itself."

Scott was a fan of the centers at first: "I spent a lot of effort on them and we hired some great people who became managers and ultimately leaders in the company. And then we started to run into a few little issues: we got trainees placed in stores, but the managers didn't have a role in hiring them, didn't know them very well, and felt like we were forcing people on them." In the end, the company decided to decentralize the program and train managers in individual districts and regions.

Today, Tom Ellison is one of the few people in the company who feels it might have been a mistake to close the Orem and Cambridge centers. "They were costing us maybe a million and a half bucks per year. It was a lot of money to run them, but in hindsight I think we threw the baby out with the bath water." Late in the 1990s, he argues, there were too-few managers trained to handle the continuing corporate growth – "we didn't have the bench that we had built from those training centers."

GANG OF FOUR AND BLACK TUESDAY

But that problem was a few years away. There were other pressing challenges that reared up earlier in the decade. In 1993 Scott and Mike Griffith were feeling so unappreciated that they were prepared to leave the company and set up their own thrift-store operations elsewhere. "Scott and I were the ringleaders," Mike says. "We wanted to have more say and more money."

John Bacon picks up the story: "They'd had a meeting beforehand and I got a call in the morning, I think from Scott, and they told me that they wanted to have a meeting with Tom and me because they were quitting. Literally, I felt ill; it felt like somebody had just died. I didn't have a sense that this was going on. I was very surprised because I didn't feel that I *wasn't* giving them responsibility or credit. I think that they didn't feel that they were getting what they deserved and it was kind of a wake-up call."

Tom: "Mike and Scott came to John and me and just said, 'We're leaving the company.' We were completely caught unaware. They took great pains to say: 'There are no hard feelings, but we really feel that we need a piece of the action and we haven't gotten that. And so we have made plans with a person in Utah who is going to be our money man.' They were going someplace far away from us and were doing things in a classy way. But they were mentally gone and they expected us to say 'Good riddance' – but we said, 'Wait a minute, let's talk about this.'"

Mike: "Tom said, 'We won't accept your resignation.' We told them, 'You owners need to give us more responsibility and listen to us more.'"

Tom: "We talked about it for a better part of a week and promised them some level of phantom stock [incentive compensation crediting an employee with a hypothetical number of shares in the company] or deferred compensation – something that would give them some owner-ship in the business. We realized at that point that we'd been deficient. Not so much with Rod VanLeeuwen because he had a [compensation] plan that could get him there, but Mike Bacon was not part and parcel of that. So we put the four of them in the same group because we felt that they were leaders in the company and we started calling them the leader-ship team." (Bill Fraser, then vice-president of strategic planning, was not happy about the development and referred to the group – Rod, Scott, and the two Mikes – as "the Gang of Four").

Mike Bacon: "Both Mike and Scott had been at the end of their rope. They weren't enjoying life as much at work, but I was still okay. I was part of their team and we were driving the success of this company through grunt work. Tom and John said they'd set up a new deferred-compensation program. Each year, if we met our targets we'd get a fairly substantial percentage put into an account and each year, with interest, it would compound. It was a great deal. It's my nest egg."

The foursome all became vice-presidents and, although Walter Scott hadn't been involved in the uprising, Tom approached him one day in the company parking lot and said he was promoting Walt from director to VP of real estate. "And by the way," he added, "I'm raising your pay – I'm not paying you enough."

Summing up, Mike Griffith says: "Tom and the family opened up the company's books more. [Our action] was poorly executed, but the end result was good. The four of us were very close to the business out in the field and were passionate about it. We formed this group and Tom and Bill Fraser got involved. We all got on the same team and had phe-nomenal growth for the next few years."

In 1994, though, there was another glitch in management – what some people came to call Black Tuesday. The leadership team had been hearing complaints from people in the field, especially store managers, about the rising cost of Savers' general and administrative (G&A) expenses. G&A are the overhead expenses of operating a business not directly linked to a company's products or services. Each individual store in the chain had to pay its share of this cost back to the company, a figure based on a percentage of the store's sales. "Our G&A had been running historically around five per cent of sales in years past," Tom explains, "but we'd grown to a point that it was running closer to eight per cent of sales – and it was just out of control. It felt like we were becoming too big a company – and we wanted to get rid of a lot of those expenses. But we screwed it up in terms of the message we were delivering. If we were smart, we could have done it over three or four months and said, 'Here's our goal and here's how we want to go about doing that.'"

Instead, district and store managers and department heads from corporate office were brought together for a workshop session with executive-leadership consultant Bill Maynard of The Effectiveness Institute, of Redmond, Washington. There were bonding exercises, a forum where managers related personal stories, and a collective defining of corporate values. At one point, Tom rose to announce that he didn't like the direction the company was going and would be cutting the expenses of departments that didn't directly generate revenue.

Buddy Grimmett was there as director of one of those departments: loss prevention. "We were all told about the cuts and would have the chance to come back the next day to make a compelling argument about why we shouldn't be cut. I was too dense to realize it was a done deal. I had to terminate four of my people and another two became store managers."

Some participants found the public process painful to watch, Jeff Smail among them. While agreeing that much head-office waste was trimmed at the workshop (among the casualties was the Orem training center), he says "Buddy was up there fighting for survival. I felt bad about that." Canadian district manager Mike Davison was one of those who nicknamed the process Black Tuesday. "I told Tom that I liked what he did, but I wouldn't have done it there in front of all of us. He should have taken these people back to the corporate office and then done what he had to do."

"We didn't lay off many at all, but we scared people a lot," Tom admits now. "We messed it up in the terms of how we communicated. No one would argue that the business decisions we made were wrong. It was the way that we went about doing it and the way that people felt about it. It was just a sophomoric way of delivering a company message."

CHOOSING THE CHARITIES

A few months after Black Tuesday, Tom asked Buddy to get involved in vendor relations. "People don't understand why we have to take care of our charities," he told Buddy. "You have to be the voice for the charities."

Looking at the work the Big Brothers Big Sisters organizations and Northwest Center in Seattle were doing, Buddy says, "I started to get a feel for what this family was giving back to these non-profits. I loved this family, I loved what they stood for." Under Rod's direction he began to work with Wayne Penner to negotiate with charities in the U.S. Buddy's first approach, to Friends of National Multiple Sclerosis Society in Reno, was "a total debacle." The female executive director told him how her charity was suffering financially in its partnership with Savers. He told her: "It's because of your inefficiencies." She called Wayne and Tom and wrote a letter of complaint. "I said, 'I'm not sure I'm cut out for this,'" Buddy relates, "and I sent Wayne in to smooth things over." Fortunately, the executive director resigned shortly after and Savers offered the non-profit a raise of twenty-five cents per OK, which turned the organization around. And a few months later, Tom said: "Give them a fifty-cent raise. We're doing very well with that store and we can share that with them." As Buddy reflected years later, "It just reinforced to me that by being fair – giving a raise in mid-contract for no reason – that you can accomplish a lot of things."

He often felt like Santa Claus approaching charities to supply stores in new areas of the U.S. He'd assure them: "We will financially back you for one year. We'll set you up in this business and guarantee you will not lose one dime and make a minimum of $25,000. We'll train the employees, hire the manager, financially guarantee the trucks that are needed – and at the end of one year, if you want to walk away, you just have to throw me the keys and you're off the hook. By the way, I'm going to pay all your gas and the insurance." And he would give them references from other non-profits working with the company.

That's how Savers signed up Big Brothers Big Sisters in Alaska and Massachusetts – where he had to convince separate branches to work together in Boston – Easter Seals in Wisconsin, epilepsy organizations in Minnesota, and the El Paso, Texas, branch of Candlelighters Childhood Cancer Foundation. One group that caused some concern at first was Safe Nest, an advocacy group running a crisis hot line and emergency shelter for battered women (and men) in Las Vegas. While the company preferred to partner with politically neutral groups, Buddy made the case for this organization to Tom: "We have to look at how groups fit in with the local environment. If we want to do a gay organization in San Francisco, it would probably work – but it wouldn't in the Bible Belt. A domestic-violence organization in Las Vegas works, with all the gambling and alcohol abuse in Sin City." Recalling the pitch later, Buddy said, "I don't know if Tom embraced this with open arms, but he didn't shut me down." Safe Nest is still linked with Savers today.

IN THE LAND OF OZ

In Canada, Savers' continuing rich relationship with Canadian Diabetes would spark further synergy in the 1990s. Early in the decade, executives from Diabetes Australia had come to a world conference in Winnipeg, learned about CDA's link with Savers, and visited Village stores in the Manitoba capital. Tom recalls: "Something like this looked like a silver bullet to the Australians and they wanted to get involved, too. So they started writing and calling: 'Come see us, there's nobody like you in Australia.'"

He and John Bacon flew over in 1992 and discovered that was true. The country did have something called charity-owned "op shops" (for "opportunity"), popular since the late 1980s, but they were often disorganized and didn't open in the evening. "We spent two weeks there in

A store in the multicultural Brunswick area of Melbourne, launched in 1997, was the first Savers operation in Australia – leading to four more outlets.

quality time driving around the four biggies – Brisbane, Melbourne, Adelaide, and Sydney – and met with each of the chief executives of the state diabetes organizations in Queensland, Victoria, New South Wales, and South Australia. But over the next year we were launching a lot of stores in North America and had a bunch of other initiatives happening. We just could not handle Australia at that point. Still, I had the fire burning from the time I saw that group of cities and John was equally as impressed – so we knew we were going back someday."

They'd met an engineer in Melbourne named Roger Wise through his brother-in-law, a store manager at a Vancouver Village. Over the next two years Roger trained from time to time at the Orem Center and in three Canadian stores, with the idea of being involved in an Australian startup. In 1996 the fire in Tom's belly flared up and a plan to launch in the Victoria capital of Melbourne (population: 3.1 million) began to take shape. Roger was named general manager of Australian operations; Craig Rasmussen, an Ontario district manager with a dozen years' Savers experience, became operations manager; and Wayne Penner, who had stream-lined the charities' phone solicitations in North America, came to organize a similar operation in Australia.

Wayne noticed many differences: "It was my first time in Australia, driving on the left-hand side of the road, doing roundabouts the wrong way, and always getting in trouble speeding. We were very successful, but the government made us pay outrageous rates for telephone reps – $14 an hour. Fortunately, the production there was double the U.S. We were getting fourteen promises of donations an hour using a manual dialling system."

"The big difference in Australia," says Tom, "is that the expense structure is so high. Payroll, for starters, is double what it is in North America where, at the end of the day, unions are just businesses. In Australia they're more ingrained in society. And then the expense to generate merchandise there is higher – although it certainly isn't double because there was already a huge recycling program in place with a lot of different charities using drop boxes."

John had his own problems getting the first store physically up and running: "It was a semi-industrial building, not a retail building, and had no parking so we basically had to reshape the whole thing. In a lot of cases we had to buy fixtures in the U.S. and send them by container because they didn't have anything like them there. We had to containerize almost the whole store. We essentially designed it, ordered stuff built, brought it down, and assembled it. There were only a few things that we did on-site; it was a big challenge just trying to get the basic fundamentals."

The store opened in November 1997 in Brunswick, an inner-north-ern Melbourne suburb where nearly half the residents speak a language other than English in the home (and where the multiculturalism lends color each year during an annual party on Sydney Road, the street where the store's located).

Over the next two years Roger, with no retail background, faded out of the picture as Craig became Australian regional manager, opening four more stores around Melbourne. The last one was in the blue-col-lar and increasingly multicultural Footscray, the unofficial capital of Mel-bourne's western suburbs (which boisterously celebrates the Vietnamese New Year). The grand opening set a three-day Australian sales record of

$87,500. As hopeful as that figure was, the stores Down Under would languish for a few years to come.

LONELY AT THE TOP

The company had kept spreading geographically through the 1990s: across the U.S. in Colorado, South Dakota, North Dakota, Missouri, Ohio, Florida, Rhode Island, Massachusetts, and New York state; and in the Atlantic Canada provinces of Nova Scotia, New Brunswick, and Newfoundland. In 1995 the hundredth store opened in Mount Vernon, Washington. Typically, John Bacon had gone up the day before and made the staff reposition the interior signs. At the opening ceremony, Tom proudly handed the store key to his father, who recalls: "I was on Cloud 9. It was the goal I'd set years before: if we can do one store, we can do ten; if we can do ten, we can do a hundred."

The growth was good and lucrative for much of the decade – until about 1998. The speed of Savers' expansion was pressuring Tom and, as president, he was feeling literally lonely at the top. Earlier in the decade, he says, "we were very much on our game. A big part of us succeeding then – with the momentum carrying into late '97 – was driven by the fact that we were working hard. We were plugged in totally. John Bacon was plugged into the U.S., Rod into Canada, and I was both places all of the time. I lived on the road, I was their partner, they were my partner. Going into a new market, we knew it extremely well before we opened our first store. We had a very hands-on connection with the first not-for-profit supplier. We picked good store locations and from 1987 Walter Scott [vice-president of real estate] became our dealmaker extraordinaire with a lot of experience in both the U.S. and Canada – he's been everywhere and all these deals have his signature on them.

"By the time we started to fail in about late '96, I had spent years with Rod going through Canada and picking locations; we became one on how we were doing this. It used to be I saw every single store before it opened, approved every site. Scott [Blomquist] was running the upper Midwest and picking sites. But of the half-dozen sites that opened in '98, some still do not make money or we've closed them – sites that were selected without an approval process in place. We believed – and still believe – operations people should be presented sites and then they should make the selection.

"The other big problem was we stopped having a dedicated local supply when the first store opened in a new area. We started shipping merchandise across state lines. We built huge supply sites in Long Island, New York, Boston, and Minneapolis, where we generated tons of excess merchandise that we'd planned to shift to different places across the country. They were great distribution centers, but it cost a lot of money – into the millions – to move this merchandise to these places. Then we found that we couldn't be successful with only shipped-in goods [as opposed to also supplying stores with locally collected merchandise]. And that's when we realized that we needed to cut that back.

"These were all huge departures in what was our very important three-legged stool of success, which is a great store location, great management ready to run the store, and a great supplier locally. If you are missing one of the three, then you will not succeed – and in some cases we had only one of them.

"Had I stayed dedicated to being on the road all of the time, I probably could have kept up a while longer, but we didn't have the team necessary to continue the growth at the rate we were growing. I should have been grooming a direct successor for me and the right real-estate people to select these locations.

"John had been very plugged in up until about 1996 and then he started to lose interest in being involved in the day-to-day grind. I think a good deal of that was because of the management change that we made in '94 – making him feel redundant. His interest in store design remained, but his interest in actually being on the ground in different cities all the time waned. And so by '99 it was clear to me that both John and my dad were ready to sell out."

Mike Griffith offers a hard-headed view of what was happening at the time: "We had pretty well reached saturation in Canada – that fast, easy, profitable growth was drying up. In the U.S. every market we opened up had competition, and we made a strategic error in getting too spread out in far-flung areas and couldn't support the stores."

A shrewd observer in the corporate office points out that the leadership team had become "the dysfunctional Gang of Four – they'd meet every Monday and nothing would come to any coherent action plan because they were always split. Two would have an opinion on things and two would disagree." In 1998 the leadership team was disbanded.

"We were just chasing our tail," Mike says. "The company was too big for our management team. You looked up and all of a sudden you're in twenty-six states, nearly ten provinces, with seven thousand employees and $300 million in sales. So if you made a mistake, it was a big mistake. And we barely were budgeting. Tom became convinced that the management team – us – could not do the job anymore. I agreed with that thinking. We had nobody on this team that had operated a company that size before. Everybody here had reached the Peter Principle" – the theory that employees reach their highest level of competence and then get promoted and remain at a level where they're incompetent.

Tom – stretched to his limit – would include himself in that definition. "Hiring a president, forming a board of directors, and taking in a partner were all things that I felt this company needed to protect itself against a disaster – which might include me and one or two other key executives going down in a plane or whatever. There was no succession plan. One of our collective family shortcomings was not having successors in all areas of the company.

"So by late '98 I was feeling a little lonely. I was feeling that the company was unprotected if something happened to me. And I just knew that after me doing it for fourteen years, someone else could bring some new ideas to the game. What I didn't know was how complicated that process would be."

Once again, the time had come to start passing it on.

"It was absolutely out of the question to sell the company."

THE PRICE OF PROGRESS

CHAPTER EIGHT

It's been called everything from the world's best consulting service to a secret international society of capitalists. The Young Presidents' Organization (YPO) is really just a way for its members – corporate presidents below age forty – to become better executives through networking, education, and the exchange of ideas. Tom Ellison joined YPO in late 1996. "It completely changed my point of view," he recollects. "We'd built this company very much from the inside. We could only see what was going in our own world, but when I joined YPO, I learned a lot about other businesses and how they capitalized them. At first I felt I was just a little 'junk' merchant and what could I offer? What did we have that was better than anybody else? What I then realized was how complicated our company was compared to a lot of others. Today we have a tremendous far-flung network of stores, dealing with non-profits and with tax systems in three countries. And we'd been able to grow without having to take on partners. But there were a lot of things that we didn't know."

It was at a local YPO chapter meeting that Tom met Jeff Schoenfeld, a Seattle entrepreneur who'd started an online travel booking service and a successful corporate travel agency (now owned by Expedia Inc.). In late 1998 Jeff introduced him to his brother-in-law, Randy Ottinger, who was joining YPO. Randy, after holding senior positions in the telecommunications-software field for more than twenty years, became a vice-president of the Bank of America's private bank. When Tom mentioned to him that he'd been approached by two private-equity firms about buying Savers,

Opposite: In 1998 Tom Ellison began contemplating the options for Savers' future.

Tom hired Lea Anne Ottinger, a female pioneer in the leveraged-buyout industry, as the company's director of corporate finance and mergers and acquisitions.

and other people suggested taking it public, Randy said, "Talk to my wife, Lea Anne. This was her career. Just pick her brain."

Lea Anne Ottinger and her husband are directors of the Ottinger Foundation, a private family funder of non-profit organizations that promote innovative policies and citizen activism "to build a movement for change." Seattle-reared, she majored in American studies at Stanford University (where she once work-shadowed Condoleezza Rice, a political-science professor who became President George W. Bush's National Security Advisor – "the most extraordinary woman I'd ever met," Lea Anne says). In 1982, at age twenty-three, she joined the Thomas H. Lee Company, a creative venture-capital enterprise in Boston. At the time, she had no idea what a leveraged buyout was but would become a female pioneer in the industry and a junior partner in the company. She later helped found Berkshire Partners, a private-equity investment firm in Boston. In her eight-year financial career Lea Anne completed dozens of acquisitions in the $25 million to $400 million range. "What distinguished Berkshire was the desire to invest in growth companies instead of plain old smoke-stack-America ones."

The concept of change has never been a barrier to Lea Anne. In 1990 she and her husband returned to Seattle to raise a family – they have three children – and acquired several franchises of The Body Shop, the worldwide hair and body-care retailer. The chain, created by Anita Roddick in England, pursues social and environmental change. "And it was a life-changing experience for me," Lea Anne says. "It's the real deal in terms of social consciousness."

She and Tom, meeting for a coffee next door to Savers at the Bellevue Club, hit it off from the get-go. "She is a very smart person," he says. And enthusiastic and attractive. "To me," Lea Anne says, "the company was absolutely dynamic. They were coming off a ten-year period of twenty-per-cent compound annual growth in both sales and earnings. I saw it as an adolescent company; there was nobody with experience to take it to the next level. Tom and John were great partners with different strengths in their heyday. And Rod was an important part of that team, but he was ready to take a lesser role. Tom and I both came up with the same idea, which was why didn't I come aboard as an independent consultant?" By December 1998 she'd become a director of corporate finance and mergers and acquisitions.

A few months into the process, Tom and Lea Anne decided to select an investment bank to help cast a wider net for suitors to invest in Savers. Of about four possibilities, they chose Donaldson, Lufkin & Jenrette (DLJ), which serves institutional, corporate, government, and high-net-worth clients. "Here's our financial statements, our balance sheet, here's what we look like and who we are," Tom told them. "Take a deep dive into this world of ours and tell us what you think our options are to sustain this business and enhance it."

The options, they told him, were to go public, or recapitalize the business himself – which meant he would be buying out his father and John Bacon – or recapitalize with a private-equity partner, or simply make a strategic sale of the company. "It was quick and easy for me to rule out things. Number one: absolutely out of the question to sell the company because I couldn't control what could happen to our team members. I wouldn't be able to protect the people at the corporate office, we could potentially lose our identity, and I did not want to leave the business. I ruled out going public because public retail companies get no respect, and the new set of rules after the Enron disaster [the high-flying American energy company collapsed into bankruptcy] make being a public company a massive pain. So it came down to recapitalize a loan or recapitalize

Ellen Spiess, the assistant corporate secretary, helped Mike Griffith prepare for negotiations that would lead to finding a partner for the company.

with a strategic partner. I like collaboration. Maybe that's not my reputation but deep down that is really true.

"At the time, there were about 200 private-equity firms out there with a collective $200 billion to invest in companies. I said, 'I'm not sold on this process, but find me the firms that have specific retail experience'– and the bank came back with a list of names" – seventy-nine of them in the first go-round.

Observing the process, and assisting with some of the details, was Ellen Spiess, the assistant corporate secretary and field communications manager. An interesting character, this native of Washington has no compunction revealing that she became an alcoholic (like Bill Ellison) in her twenties. Recovering, she worked a dozen years for a Seattle stevedoring company, which later formed its own insurance company, where she became manager of operations from California to Alaska. Ellen came to Savers in 1991 to help reduce the the number of workers'-compensation claims and better manage the claims that did happen. She became co-risk manager for several years before Mike Griffith approached her to work on "some highly confidential matters." These turned out to be the negotiations for a potential partnership.

"It was pretty hectic," Mike says. "Ellen and I didn't know what we were doing. All these lawyers and MBAs twenty years younger than I, and smarter. It was way over my head. We went on a road show and did these presentations to big banks, which I'm terrible at. Tom had never been through it – but he just shone."

Tom describes his confidant Mike as "very intelligent, one of the few people that looked outside the company a lot besides me." Ellen agrees: "Mike is highly intelligent – he knows so much about so many things. But several of us had what we called 'the Mike Griffith three-times-ask rule.' He'd ask you to prepare an analysis and you'd spend a lot of time doing a spreadsheet and give it to him. And he'd say: 'This is great. What's this all about?' He had no memory of asking us to do it. So we wouldn't do things the first time he asked or the second. Then if he asked you the third time, you knew he really, really wanted it. But I'd take him back as a boss in a heartbeat."

Ellen could see that Tom needed help in running the mushrooming company: "I believe at the time he felt like he'd given all he had to give. John [Bacon] wasn't here very much. There was no active board [just family members]. They'd have maybe one meeting a year – a barbecue and then they'd write up the minutes." She welcomed Lea Anne Ottinger's involvement: "She's brilliant – and so much fun. She really knew the investment business and Tom trusted her."

The process continued through October and November 1999. Eventually only nineteen of the seventy-nine groups the investment bank had identified as a prospective partner for Savers survived the first cut. That short list was pared down to eleven and then four, whose principals visited the company in Bellevue. Among them was Lea Anne's old firm, Berkshire Partners, which had initially been low on the totem pole of possible contenders. Berkshire's portfolio companies include a British rail-freight company and Acosta, North America's single largest consumer packaged goods sales and marketing agency. But it has also invested in retail stalwarts such as Carter's, Inc., the biggest U.S. branded marketer of young children's apparel, and MD Beauty, which develops, markets, and sells branded cosmetics and skin-care products in the healthy-beauty market.

"I liked all of them," Tom says of the quartet of candidates. "They were all potential partners – great people, great resources, smart group of folks. They had varying backgrounds. One was a very wealthy family investment firm in Rockefeller Center in New York who had money since the early 1900s that came from a steel fortune. Another was a very famous private real-estate developer in Chicago, a very colorful man who has a private-equity fund of his own and a lot of very smart people running it. Then the other two were traditional private-equity firms, a very large private one based in Chicago and Berkshire Partners in Boston. All four of them had a good pedigree in retail background."

Wanting to get to know them better, he asked the investment bankers if it was a good idea to meet the candidates on their own turf to take the measure of the various corporate cultures and see which would be the best fit. DLJ's people – relationship manager Jim Sington, mergers and acquisitions specialist Jeff Raiche, and vice-president Matthew Spain, who did the bulk of the work on the file – agreed that it was, although the move was highly unusual. Jim joined Tom and his colleagues on their trips to the three cities.

"The first meeting was in New York City with this private family firm in a very expensive office complex," Tom recounts. "And the guy who had been so warm and friendly was a different person around his team of people. Seeing him on his turf showed him up for what he really was. By the time we walked out of there, we knew it was not these guys. The next meeting was with a very flamboyant, well-known real-estate maven and, as a student of real estate, I was a bit in awe of this person. He's a multi-billionaire with a long reach. A tremendously interesting guy, but within five minutes I knew he was not going to be my partner.

"So on we moved to this other private-equity firm in Chicago, an organization much bigger than Berkshire who really know their stuff. They probably had the most interesting retail portfolio experience. They took us to Charlie Trotter's [which *Wine Spectator* magazine once named "The Best Restaurant in the World for Wine and Food"]. And Charlie Trotter is a friend of this firm's partner. We had this unbelievable meal – a $6,000 tab for dinner, including the wine. We met with them the next day and I was impressed. Overall, they were smart guys and so I didn't rule them out; I just wanted to think about it for a while.

"Then the last one was Berkshire Partners in Boston. I met them with Lea Anne and felt a certain warmness, a genuineness from these guys. They actually called a special meeting and pulled their entire firm together, including secretaries. In my first meeting with Berkshire, I'd been impressed because there was the senior partner, the junior partner,

Berkshire's Kevin Callaghan (left) and Chris Clifford are outside directors of Savers; Josh Lutzker (right) offers analytical and management support.

and the associate – the guy who does all the analysis and gets them all ready for the meeting. Well, their associate isn't a flunky. His name is Josh Lutzker [now a senior associate] and he was very vocal and very much empowered in the meeting. That spoke to me. So I liked Berkshire and now it was down to two, including the private-equity firm in Chicago. I called the past and present CEOs in the portfolio companies that each was involved with, and Mike called the CFOs of those companies. And we found that the Chicago firm was pretty autocratic. I also realized that at that point I was thinking of selling down to a point where I was only about twenty per cent of the new company – and I just did not want to give up control of the business, no matter how good my new partners were going to be."

Lea Anne: "At the eleventh hour, everybody had been talking about buying eighty per cent of the company. Then at the last moment (and this is their forté) Berkshire came up with two offers: eighty-twenty [leaving Tom only twenty per cent of the company] and the other was fifty-fifty — which was a total no-brainer, a win-win all around. It accomplished every objective. WOE and John were able to cash out, and Tom had a skin-in-the-game, intelligent partner. We had the handshake in December '99."

But there were some last-minute hitches. "Between then and May 2000, the capital markets crumbled and Berkshire's financing became a lot more complicated. And the bank suddenly started pulling in their reins. The bank negotiations were very grueling. That's when the bank put in some provisions that were a little upsetting to Tom – hard-core legal mumbo-jumbo. There were so many details that, on many occasions right up until a couple of nights before we closed the deal, Tom said, 'I don't need this. Hey, I was happy when I had fifty cents in my pocket.' But when it closed, he said, 'I'm really glad I did this.'"

Starting in May 2000, Tom shared ownership equally with a well-financed partner that has experience with other retail chains and that values its relationship with a thrift department-store chain. As Berkshire reported in a recent year-end summary of its operations:

> Savers enjoys a dominant position in the for-profit thrift retail market and has demonstrated resistance to economic downturns during the last few years. The company has a reputation for providing an attractive value proposition to its customers and significant revenue to its non-profit partners, all of which contribute to an exceptional track record of profitable growth. Savers and Berkshire continue to pursue opportunities to grow the business via new store openings and acquisition.

"The epilogue," Tom says now, "is that Berkshire is everything I thought they would be – and more. They are very caring, very good people to work with, and we have never referred to the agreement that took us so long to negotiate in the process. They had the right to pick half the outside board members and I had the right to pick the other half. I picked them all – that's just the way they are."

The board today includes Tom as chairman and Rod VanLeeuwen and Lea Anne as directors. (Rod also acts as an executive advisor on planning, development, real estate, and building layouts.) Other voting members are *John Meisenbach*, president of MCM, a Seattle financial-services company, who serves on the boards of Costco Companies Inc., Expeditors International, Acorto, and McCormick Capital Management; *Arthur Rubinfeld*, an architect and the founder and president of Airvision Advisory Group, consultants specializing in the development of operational plans, brand positioning, and growth strategies, and former executive VP of Starbucks Coffee Company; *Kevin Callaghan*, managing director of

Berkshire Partners, formerly with Lehman Brothers providing corporate-finance and acquisition advisory services; and *J. Christopher Clifford*, a Berkshire managing director and a former partner in the Thomas H. Lee Company.

One former Savers executive who didn't go on the board was John Bacon, who effectively retired to run his own small company, which builds and redevelops apartment buildings and houses. A board member kept asking John if he'd be interested in becoming a director. "And Tom sort of asked me, but it more or less died," John says. "I was reluctant about being on the board because I was afraid I'd have opinions and see or hear things that were happening and I'd have no control over them. When you have a keen sense of ownership, there's a lot of emotions you have."

To this day, Tom says, "I would still like to get him involved in the company. John has a design sense. Our stores need a new look. John could be really valuable in that process. But the game is not over. He could get back involved if he really wanted to make a move."

John had spent his entire career with the company (and his son John D. Bacon followed him, working for thirteen years in stores and information technology). Reflecting on his retirement, he admits, "I haven't been in a store since. I loved it there."

BRASH NEW BROOMS

The other hitches in the forward progress of the freshly refashioned Savers were longer-term and much more profound in their impact. Just before the partnership deal closed, Berkshire recommended a chief financial officer in his fifties from Amarillo, Texas. It had hired Dennis McGill for six months to turn around a troubled company operating gift stores on cruise-ship lines. Based on his success there, Berkshire's people suggested him as a financially savvy executive vice-president for Savers.

"I met Dennis and liked him," Tom recalls. "He was never going to be the president of the company, but he had skill as a CFO and I started to give him more and more responsibility." Rod VanLeeuwen says Dennis did want to be the CEO someday and while "he brought some good things in with him, he was driven and would drive others past the point where it would do good. Culturally, he wasn't the best fit." Among his innovations, Dennis created a global team intended to create a communications link among all the individual "silos" of activity in the company. It was a good idea badly executed, Tom says. A new compensation program Dennis introduced, offering a system of bonuses but tinkering with pension plans, was greeted with hostility throughout the company – "it was an absolute nightmare," says Brenda Seraphim, the Canadian human-resources director.

The personable and dynamic Gary White, who became Savers' new CEO, had a background with the retail giants Target, Mervyn's, and Gymboree.

Morale improved at first with the next senior executive Tom hired. Gary White was a gregarious and inspirational Cleveland-reared executive who'd started his career with a local discount department store and then became a store manager for Target, the large-store, general-merchandise discount chain. By 1990 he'd advanced to the post of regional VP and grew with the rapidly expanding company, launching a training program called Target University. He later moved as executive VP of stores and operations to Target's subsidiary Mervyn's, a middle-market department-store group in the west and south. In 1997 the forty-four-year-old left to be the new senior VP and chief operating officer of Gymboree, a troubled California-based chain specializing in play programs and retail children's clothing in four countries.

Two years later the magazine *Black Enterprise* praised Gary White, by now CEO, for leading a thirty-per-cent growth and expansion initiative that had put Gymboree ahead of its leading competitor and only second to the Gap in sales. The article noted his idea of reserving five seats on the board of directors for kids aged four and five and concluded: "This forward, innovative thinking proves that Gymboree is in very capable hands and White will soon have the most toys in the sandbox."

It was only a year later that the *San Francisco Chronicle* was reporting: "Amid hemorrhaging sales, Gymboree Corp.'s chief executive, Gary White . . . resigned under pressure yesterday."

A few months later, he surfaced on Savers' radar screen. After a fruitless six-month search, Tom Ellison and Lea Anne Ottinger had failed to find a suitable candidate to replace Tom as CEO. Then a headhunter suggested Gary as a real possibility.

"He'd lasted as Gymboree's CEO for about a year and then something happened," Tom remembers. "We tried and tried in the reference-checking to talk to the chairman of the company and find out what really happened, but there was no information. But we had good feedback from the Target people. The guy is charming and is a very effective communicator. So we made the decision to hire Gary."

At the start, in November 2000, he presented well. As Ellen Spiess noticed shrewdly from her catbird seat in corporate office, "When he started, Tom gave him the keys to the company. Gary was a tremendously charismatic person – he made you feel you were the most important person in the world. He'd sit in a cubicle with a team member and ask him how his day was going. He was good at creating teams and making you feel you wanted to make the company better. But in his presentation of an idea, you'd get so caught up in his enthusiasm that you maybe didn't understand that it was a *bad* idea. An example was that he wanted walls of merchandise up to eight feet high to make the stores so jam-packed. But it was hard to display and access the merchandise. They may have done that at Target, but it didn't work for us. And he didn't take criticism very well. He would not take the advice of Tom and Rod and the board. Meanwhile, there was so much unrest and fear in the field. He really forced people to look at sub-performers and there was a lot of turnover at that time."

All of which Tom agrees with: "While I knew we had a very intense and unique culture in the company, I never really knew how deep it went until I watched someone single-handedly start to dismantle it – which is what Gary did. He didn't want to collaborate with the board. It was very much new against old: none of the old guard had any good ideas. He thought the model was broken and wanted to change it completely. He didn't do experiments in one store or five stores, he did them in the entire company. We do four fifty-per-cent-off sales a year in Canada, six in the United States, and he expanded that to a total of eighteen days. It's crazy how busy the stores get on sales days, the people wipe us out of merchandise, and it's not tremendously profitable."

Another of Gary's experiments was the third attempt in Savers' history to introduce new merchandise in the stores – in this case, discounted dollar-store goods. It didn't work. Long ago, when Tom joined the company, his father had set a goal of having new items make up half the stock in the stores. That idea eventually died, only to be resurrected in the late 1980s for a few years. Today, the only new merchandise that has proven to pay off throughout the chain is geared to the Halloween season.

"But the most important thing," Tom argues, "was that Gary didn't really want to talk about things – he just did them, his way. During his tenure we had a hundred U.S. stores and we lost over fifty per cent of store managers – either they got fired or they quit.

"Dennis McGill at first was very much trying to be the person that he knew I wanted him to be: a leader, yet interactive. But when I hired Gary, Dennis became a different person and was tremendously hard on people. I had to force Gary to fire Dennis – whom he liked because Dennis did his dirty work for him. And I'm not sure my Berkshire partners were comfortable with that. They weren't on the ground to see the kind of damage Dennis was doing, but you could see it in the numbers. The company was in trouble."

During Gary's tenure, a team of engineers analyzed the processes used in the stores' production rooms. Then the company began implementing an EZ-Flow system, based on existing "best practices" in place at some outlets. It was an attempt to create a consistent, corporate-wide process – from how to position a rolling rack of clothes most efficiently to how many staples to use in attaching a tag to an item. At the time, Shannon Givens told employees, "EZ-Flow will do just what it says: make your job easier, and keep our stores cleaner and more organized. It's just one of the projects that will help us achieve the vision that Gary White has laid out for us."

In truth, Shannon had a mixed reaction to Gary, who promoted her to vice-president and managing director of Canadian operations: "He was a very intelligent man with a lot of experience and knowledge. But he was extremely impatient and he chewed through people fast because of that impatience. I didn't have a lot of challenges with Gary, as a lot of people in the company had . . . Gary really didn't say No to me on a lot on things that I wanted to do and I really understood what he was trying to accomplish. He was just doing it too fast. Gary was so hard on people and we lost so many management people in the U.S. We lost a lot of the tricks of the trade with them. We became very focused on meeting quotas and numbers as opposed to quality."

Tom: "The last three or four months that Gary was here, it was a revolving door. People were just leaving, leaving, leaving, and he didn't see that Rome was burning. We opened a store in Revere, Massachusetts, and at a real-estate committee meeting I asked Gary point-blank if he had management to run this store. 'Oh yeah, we will have management on the ground,' he said. Well, we hired a store manager *two weeks* before the store opened. No one can possibly know this business in that period of time. That is how bad things were. Our profits were dropping, our comparable store sales were in the minus category for the first time ever. It was a mess. But the board – me included – was reticent about really going after the issue, afraid that we would chase Gary out the door. Then Lea Anne and I started to ring the emergency bell."

"Gary White is one of the most attractive individuals you'll ever meet," Lea Anne Ottinger concedes. "But Gary wanted to bring Target to Savers without really understanding Savers. He managed too much by fear, and we lost too many people and too much knowledge too fast."

It wasn't only some team members who feared him. In March 2002 the principals of charities supplying the company with merchandise were dumbstruck by a sudden, unilateral action he sprang on them.

As Tom tells it, "Buddy Grimmett was running the sourcing department at that time and overall was doing a pretty good job, although he understood there were certain shortcomings in his organization." Gary, meanwhile, didn't know what to do with Scott Blomquist. After the leadership team had dissolved, Scott moved into operations and was opening and overseeing stores in the southeastern U.S. When Gary appointed himself head of stores, he made Scott head of sourcing, also known as vendor relations, a move that demoted Buddy to an assistant's role – although he soon returned to his previous loss-prevention position.

Scott was promoted only a week before Savers invited key charity suppliers to Seattle for an annual retreat and their Partners Advisory Board meeting. Gary was adamant about cutting the cost of the OKs – the bags of merchandise – that the non-profits were providing. The company was then paying them an average of just under $9 per OK. There was talk of dropping it immediately to as low as $4 per OK. Buddy, for one, had been protesting such a move – "You don't understand how we work with our partners" – while suggesting that Gary take a slower, more deliberate approach to lowering costs.

But the new CEO, listening to the beat of his own drummer, insisted on delivering the bad news to the charity officials at their meeting. Or rather, that Scott deliver it. As Tom recalls, "Gary told him: 'You're going to get up and tell them that we need a $5 OK.' Nothing about how we might do that or if it's even possible. I don't think Gary even understood or knew. We realized we were paying too much compared to others in the industry and had to get some cost-savings measure in place. But he never talked to me or anybody else about the efficacy of what he was proposing. I was there when Scott got up and scared the living daylights out of the audience – including me. That was the beginning of the end anyway. At that point, Gary was a couple of months from his departure."

The $5 OK never materialized. Gary White left Savers in mid-May, eighteen months after he'd arrived.

A MAN FOR THE JOB

A few days later, Tom and Rod asked Ellen Spiess to give them her thoughts on Gary's departure. In a long memo she posed many questions that were disturbing her, including these: "Are we going back to the way it was before? Is Gary just a sacrifice? Discarded before the efforts that the teams have been working so hard on get a chance to blossom? Or will those things ever blossom on the current path? I don't know the answer – do you? What will your plan be?... I'm feeling very 'green' and naive – have we all been taken advantage of?... I won't pretend to know what the direction has been in individual department meetings. The plan seemed sound; the results have been dismal... I think Gary's departure will rock the company at a time when the existing stability is incredibly fragile."

Even before Gary left, Tom and Rod had been asking each other if they were prepared to take back the corporate reins. They were – while recognizing that the leave-taking of two top executives *had* rocked Savers. "Some were still very loyal to Gary," Tom believes, "and probably were scared to death that Tom and Rod were coming back in. But I would think that this melted fairly quickly because we became a tight team with a purpose very quickly. The purpose was to simplify the process. We were simply interested in people – the retention and training of people – and the production process of the stores. And right away we got rid of the new-merchandise idea that Gary had built although we kept one of the buyers he had hired."

"I've never seen anybody right the *Titanic*," Lea Anne says, "but Tom and Rod turned this ship on a dime. They went back to the basics." Rod had become a part-time executive advisor after Gary arrived. Now he came back full-time to assume the president's role on a temporary basis. He and Tom knew they had to find a permanent leader. But, not wanting to repeat the mistake they'd made with Gary White, they decided to call in an expert to help weigh the psychological cast of each serious contender. Art Resnikoff was then a forensic psychologist (developing profiles of people based on human behavior and motivation) with the California-based Hagberg Consulting Group, which specializes in leadership development and pre-hire assessment. Front-runners for the Savers position had to complete a two-hour personality and leadership profile with hundreds of statements, such as "I find I can think better when I have the advice of others," and rate them on a scale from "extremely characteristic" to "extremely uncharacteristic." As Tom explains, "It's a tough process. Art gives them the questionnaire and then interviews them for four hours. You can't really hide the person that you are in that time."

Tom had interviewed several candidates before meeting with an unlikely-sounding possibility: Ken Alterman, a general manager with the Pepsi-Cola Bottling Group in Seattle. "I'd seen Ken's resumé originally and rejected it, based on his apparent skill-set on paper," Tom says. On first glance, it's true, Ken didn't seem the ideal cultural fit. He was applying for a post with what until recently had been a tight family business – while all of his career had been with major multinationals like Pepsico.

Born in Manhattan, Ken lived as a youngster one block away from Yankee Stadium (as this baseball buff likes to tell people) and then moved with his family to Long Island. He was the middle son of a history-teacher father and an office-administrator mother. At a technical college amid the state's Adirondack Mountains, he studied chemical engineering with a focus on nuclear energy After graduating he signed up with Procter & Gamble's manufacturing management program to work as a process-improvement engineer. Instead Ken became a twenty-one-year-old supervisor in P&G's Staten Island warehouse of goods such as Tide, Crisco, and Duncan Hines cake mixes. With a job almost entirely people-oriented, he learned labor relations quickly after the workers once locked this young pup in his office overnight. The company promoted him first as a mechanical manager working with skilled licensed tradespeople and then the overseer of a startup product called Citrus Hill orange juice, which had a good launch.

In 1983, after nearly five years with the company, he was ripe for a call from Pepsico. The beverage giant hired him as a divisional technical-services manager, a liaison role with franchise bottlers in the southern division in Atlanta. Within two years he was bottler operations manager, after three the manager of the Pittsburgh plant, and eventually director of manufacturing for Pennsylvania and West Virginia. By now he'd married his high-school sweetheart, Jennifer – a math major who has been a computer programmer and a system engineer with AT&T – and they had a daughter and a son. Bruised from battling tough east-coast unions, he welcomed the chance to become director of manufacturing and operations for Pepsico in Toronto. His tasks were to lead Canadian bottlers being buffeted by cheap private-label beverages and to run the largest of all the global company's plants. There Ken and labor got along so famously that the union chief wrote his bosses a letter warning it would be a mistake to let him leave Canada.

But the American west coast called to him and his family. After a brief stint with the company in Spokane, he settled into Seattle on the sales, marketing, and advertising side. In charge of Washington state operations and supermarket-chain supplies in Oregon and Alaska, he was named market-unit manager of the year for all of Pepsico's world. His outside involvements reflected an interest in charitable and community organizations: the United Way, the Boys & Girls Club, the Corporate Council for the Arts, and the board of his synagogue. He was so reluctant to be promoted away from Seattle that he started seeking a position with a locally based enterprise. An obvious lure was Starbucks, which had a joint venture with Pepsico, but he was also intrigued with this company called Savers. He spoke with one of its directors, John Meisenbach, who suggested that Tom should meet this smart fellow named Ken Alterman.

"I interviewed him and still wasn't sure," Tom says of his first encounter with the lean-faced executive, silver-haired at forty-five. "But we then met again and I thought, *He is a pretty smart guy.* One thing about us, we're a little bit unconventional at times, and so I had never ruled him out. But I wanted to talk to a whole bunch of other people first, which I did, and then on the third interview I asked if he'd be willing to take this forensic-psychology test."

Ken was impressed with the company's financial prospects and felt he could enhance them: "The margins in the business, when the stores are run well, are quite handsome. But it appeared that Savers hit a snag in scale, and as it got bigger, it was very difficult for them to replicate the success of those first fifty stores. That seemed like a pretty good challenge for the way my brain works – both on building from the top line over the last ten years and controlling the bottom line through better process.... Just simply taking the complexity out of the business that has created inefficiency or ineffectiveness – because the top-line potential is so much greater than the cost they invested in their labor."

After his Berkshire colleagues had interviewed and approved Ken, Tom offered him an executive job – but neither the president's nor CEO's title. "You come in here with an understanding that if you are not CEO in two years, you have got to go. That said, you've got to start lower down on the food chain and establish yourself here." As Lea Anne points out, "Ken wasn't getting the title and the money and wasn't the least bit put off knowing that he'd have to earn them."

In late 2002 Ken became vice-president and general manager. He was passionate about far more than Savers' monetary potential: "I was so intrigued by the philanthropy at the outset – then how the stores are run and what they did with their waste stream – that I saw it as a real nice tight model. I love that we find opportunities to recycle, to send goods to Third World nations and reduce waste. I was taught to leave the path you cross better than you found it – and I believe that what Savers does is in keeping with that philosophy."

"Whoa! We're not taking the shoes off those kids."

A RECYCLED WORLD
CHAPTER NINE

One of the classic stories Ken Alterman would hear about Savers' recycling history had happened little more than a week after 9/11. The whole world was tense with the horror of the al-Qaeda terrorist attacks on the World Trade Center and the Pentagon, and Mike Griffith had just learned that two of Savers' employees – Phil McMullen and John Lawless – were planning a trip to West Africa. Phil was then the fifty-four-year-old director of recycling and John was the thirty-six-year-old manager of a recycling distribution center. Phoning Phil, Mike didn't know that the pair had already embarked on their journey to three African countries to meet customers for the company's vast quantity of well-used but still-usable goods. Phil picked up the call on a stopover in the Amsterdam airport. Although Mike would later agree to join him on a selling trip to India, he was hesitant about taking one to impoverished, disease-ridden, war-torn Africa. All he could say now was: "Be real careful."

John remembers stepping off the plane in Benin and being blasted by the 120-degree heat. "The air terminal is a joke – it looks like an old warehouse, with no air-conditioning – and there were probably about 300 people ahead of us trying to get into the country." Benin is a nation of 7.5 million with an average life expectancy of only fifty years and a literacy rate of forty per cent. Free elections had only happened two decades earlier; a Marxist-Leninist government was now in power. "Even calling Benin a developing country gives it more credit than it deserves. There was no running water, the pollution was unbelievable, and a gas station is a guy

Opposite: A little girl in India shows off a pair of donated shoes from America.

sitting on a corner with a wine jug full of gas."

That was John's introduction to Africa. He and Phil met a major client of Savers, who would help them contact other buyers in the next week. They drove down dirt roads to visit the street markets in Cotonou, the biggest city, with their fruits and vegetables, fabrics, musical instruments, and even voodoo objects – amulets, tree bark, and dried animals. "We walked through the markets and saw a bunch of our own merchandise, still with our tags on," he says. Among the Savers recyclables were clothes, shoes, and pots and pans sent by the container-load across the sea. The pair also showed customers two suitcases brimming with samples of other products, from books and household goods to hard and soft toys.

They next moved on to Freetown, the capital of Sierra Leone. A peace accord in the war between government and rebel forces had collapsed in May after the capture of hundreds of peacekeepers with the 17,500-man United Nations Mission in Sierra Leone. Rampant murder, limb amputations, abductions, and looting were only ending after British paratroopers freed their own and government military hostages.

Bomb-blasted roads and a bridge under rebel threat meant that Savers' team had to take an old Russian transport helicopter – "with plywood benches and duct tape literally holding it together," John says – for the short hop from the airport to their hotel, which was scarred with bullet and grenade holes. "On the plus side, it was full of UN officers, guys with machine guns all over. And Sierra Leone has the most beautiful beaches I've ever seen. I thought if they could put up hotels there, they'd be the richest country in the world." But poverty prevails, and John saw the ongoing need for recycled goods from the well-off societies of North America.

Their final stop was Lagos, Nigeria, the largest city in the largest African nation, more prosperous than the others with its strong petroleum resources. But even here, the ride from the airport took them through endless slums, past burned-out cars and open ditches draining human waste into tidal flats. After strengthening their contacts with Nigerian customers, John decided not to take his sample merchandise home with him. "I handed out a suitcase full of toys – the kids went crazy, like it was the first Christmas they ever had – and some of the kitchenware to women, who sure appreciated it. There were a couple of little kids in a house with

a dirt floor and no plumbing. I gave two pairs of little-girl-sized Nikes to their mother, and it was the first they'd ever had in their lives. The look on their faces was unbelievable."

Although John did business there, such as finding suppliers to buy used books, he flew home transformed by the emotions of his three-week experience. "It really blew my mind," he says, "to see the poverty in West Africa and what was happening to our clothes and shoes. It was a good feeling for me, making me appreciate my job; I'm not just doing this for a paycheck. There was nothing else available over there – no Payless Shoes on the corner; everything is done in markets." He came home understanding two essential facts: "Number one, the stuff we sent there was not just rotting in a garbage dump, and number two, it's being reused by people who really need it. An old iron skillet is gold. Literally, what might be considered trash here is treasure there."

John was excited about sharing his discoveries with the production staff in the Back Rooms of Savers and Value Village stores: "You're not recycling all this because you have to. It has a positive effect on other

A recycling baler packages used clothing for shipping as part of the 225 million pounds of goods that Savers distributes to developing nations annually.

people in the world. *That's* what we do." Phil had posters made and showed a video of their trip at a managers' retreat to help get this meaningful message across to the men and women in the company who can make such a difference in the lives of people a world away.

Four years later, John Lawless was general manager of recycling operations for the whole company.

RECYCLABLES, NOT RAGS

Phil McMullen, born in Seattle, studied mathematics and business at Mormon universities in Utah before starting a genealogical-research firm in Salt Lake City. In 1988, taking a large leap, he was a partner there with his brother, Wally, in Northwest Textiles, exporting mixed rags to West Africa. Graders, as businesses like this are called, sort and grade the quality of recycled used and vintage clothing and general textiles into about a hundred different categories. Then they're baled for resale to developing countries. Some is the so-called credential clothing, which has been donated directly from individuals – as it is with the product Savers receives. Grading is a profitable industry with a welcome social purpose: American landfills consist of anywhere from three to six per cent clothing and textiles that are often highly reusable by impoverished people. And charities collecting donated goods help reduce some of that waste.

But Phil always tried to be dispassionate about the industry. "The charity stops as soon as it's delivered to our door," he liked to say. "It's business every step of the way. We ship to India because we get the highest price for the goods." In 1989 the McMullens began partnering with what was then TVI, recycling the company's discards to clothing brokers or ripping and selling them as wiping cloths – rags, in the industry jargon. Northwest had more than 120 employees in plants in Salt Lake City and Tacoma. As the Tacoma manager said at the time, the major customers included Chile, which bought light cotton clothing; Pakistan, which took heavier items but asked they be wrapped in castoff blankets; and Mexico, which demanded that all price tags be removed and the clothes neatly folded. "And every month, brokers buy over 200,000 pounds of cotton garments for Africa" – which also bought leather and imitation-leather goods. Wool items, usually hard to sell, were finding buyers in India, where the yarn was reprocessed into new clothing.

In 1991 Northwest was sold to Row Clothing, a major international grading operation, and Phil went with it – although he and Row continued to handle TVI's recyclables. Six years later Phil came on staff at Savers, having convinced Rod – and then, through him, Tom – that recycling was a good and profitable in-house business. "It took about six months of convincing Rod," he says, and eventually Savers' executives stopped referring to his work as the rag business and started calling it recycling.

"When they hired me, they moved away from having the recycling division being an after-thought to where it became a major contributing part of the business financially and emotionally. They've done a good job in the last couple of years at retreats saying 'We're in the recycling business and it's part of our core business. We're willing to donate time and resources to it.'"

Phil's first challenge was the fact that there was no organized method to track the stores' receivables. He credits Mike Griffith with developing an accounting system to compare the number of OKs received to the amount of goods recycled. "One store might have a thousand OKs and generate ten pounds of mixed rags and another generates fifty pounds – five times the amount for recycling." Then the figures were fed back to the stores. "And that's what made this work. That process changed the business. People just don't want to be on the bottom of the list. When we started measuring, we had .4 pounds of shoes per OK. When I left, it was about 1.2. It wasn't because Savers was getting more shoes, but we were paying more attention to it – a three-times increase in volume of the shoes being sold and that much of a reduction going to the landfill. And the credit for that goes to Shannon: she got the stores to improve their performance."

By the time he left to form his own company in 2004, Phil had built a $25-million-a-year business within Savers and never had a signed contract with any of the company's customers – "because my word is my word." During most of that time, he felt empowered. "Tom told me there are lots of opportunities and if I worked hard, the opportunities would be endless. He never limited me to selling rags. I ran it like my own business and nobody interfered. The direction from Savers' owners was pretty minimal. Shoes is a good example. I said we ought to be selling these shoes to Africa direct rather than to a local grader – we can get four times as much money. Rod told me it was a dumb idea – 'Nobody does that in our business.'" But he gave Phil a year, along with a warehouse and funding, to make his case. The venture had sales of $800,000 in its first year; they're now about $2 million.

He had less luck in persuading the powers-that-be to get more serious about selling their used books on the Internet. John Lawless was wrestling with the concept at the time, trying to get Savers' stock on Amazon Books and eBay. He'd learned a lot from Phil, "one of the smartest guys I've ever met in this business. When it's time to get the job done, Phil's the guy. And he's not bashful. I loved having a supervisor who gives me clear direction and then lets me go do it." Phil approached Amazon himself and had software developed to link with the bookselling giant. "The tragedy," he now says of the Savers approach to the online used-book trade, "is that they were doing a lousy job of it. And that's one reason I left. They could have done a hundred times as much business."

In the end, Phil went off to launch Thrift Recycling Management,

One of the company's two recycling distribution centers – the other is in Toronto – this warehouse in Fife, Washington, is nearly 100,000 square feet.

which buys and sells shoes, mixed rags, and toys for export but makes most of its money from selling used volumes on Amazon and eBay, among other online booksellers. He took with him his son Jeff, who was supervising a team of field recycling managers, and Clive Midgen, the export sales manager. "I like building things," Phil says. "I'm not a maintenance guy. If you want to give me an impossible task, that's what I'm interested in." He did what Tom's grandfather and grand-uncle had done: "Ben Ellison and his brother left the Sally Ann because the opportunities were greater with the same skill-set, and the same thing applies to me. But I loved my time at Savers; it was a grand experience."

DUMPSTER-DIVE AUDITS

Ken Alterman soon recognized that while Phil McMullen had opened up new global markets for Savers, the company could build on – and go beyond – the recycling director's fifteen years' work. Tony Shumpert, whose background is in the freight-forwarding business, succeeded Phil as director of recycling and logistics. He oversaw John Lawless, the recycling GM, and Jonathan Licht, an online sales manager developing the Internet book trade that Phil wanted to expand. Meanwhile, Maria Kane was in charge of international sales of recyclables, traveling extensively to India and South America.

Today Savers recycles more than 225 million pounds of shoes, clothing, and kitchenware annually (not including an estimated 2 million pounds of books). Two distribution centers handle the goods that the stores have decided are either not salable enough or, if they did go on the sales floor, have not sold within a designated period of time. The larger center is in Fife, Washington, almost 100,000 square feet of product from the stores in the state's Puget Sound region as well as Salt Lake City, Phoenix, Denver, and Vancouver, B.C. In Canada a new location in the Rexdale area of Toronto, five minutes from the international airport, has more than doubled capacity to 50,000 square feet. The Canadian facility also receives items from New York's Long Island, Boston, Minnesota, Halifax, and Winnipeg. Fife handles all online book sales and more baled clothing than Toronto. As John describes the centers, "They're the cleanest, most organized, most professional mess you've ever seen."

After Jeff McMullen left with his father, John assumed the role of supervising four field managers – one in each of Toronto and Phoenix and two in the Seattle area. Two of them are former store managers. Their goal is to do at least two recycling audits of each store a year, although some outlets may need three or four to get up to speed. John tries to visit one store each quarter. He came up through the stores himself. A long-distance trucker living in El Paso, he started at Savers as an assistant manager helping to open the Tucson store in 1994. He moved five times in five years before becoming district manager for south Puget Sound. In 2000 Mike Griffith encouraged him to apply for the Fife manager's position.

Now, as general manager, he ensures that the stores are constantly evaluated according to a three-page audit form. A section on shoes, for instance, instructs the auditors: "Check the trash barrels at the Shoe station. What percentage of shoes did you find that should have either gone on the sales floor or to the recycler? If one pair found, award no points." His field managers meet with the store managers to review their recycling figures and visit each department to check whether the recycling is being done properly. "We even dumpster-dive to look for things that should have been recycled," he says. They offer individual training to employees at each station in the Back Room and then follow up with the managers to put a plan in place to correct any lapses.

Often the store staff have their own concerns. A typical one was published as a Q&A in the employee newsletter, *The Voice*:

Dear Otis: I am a miscel pricer, and almost every day I come across donations such as canned baby formula, dog food, makeup and bar soaps that are unopened, unexpired, non-perishable but unsellable (according to my manager). I've been instructed to throw them out, which I do. It pains me to see these items go into the trash instead of passing them on to other organizations like humane societies or domestic violence shelters. I've even volunteered to take these items to the shelters, but I've been told no. My question: if we really are in the business of recycling, why aren't we allowed to recycle these items? Is this my manager's decision or the company's policy? Lastly, if such a policy does exist, why not change it or ask our solicitors to mention that these types of items are useless to us so we wouldn't receive them anyway? *Sincerely, Recycle? Huh!*

Dear Recycle: This is an excellent question that comes up often and is researched and considered every time. Our policy states that food, medicinal products, and personal consumption and hygiene products are to be immediately disposed of. In the past, we have tried to offer the items we throw away to worthwhile causes, but usually they need the items presorted to certain specifications. Unfortunately, we don't have the manpower, time, or space to do this. Likewise, the non-profit organizations don't have the resources to filter out these unwanted products from donations before delivering them to our stores. It is a fine line to walk, and we must remember we are a for-profit organization and we

Jonathan Licht, who worked in magazine-distribution management
in New York and Tacoma, inherited Savers' online bookselling business
from Phil. "The concept was to figure out a way of avoiding the waste fees
of getting the product to the dump," he says. The cost of putting rejected
books into landfills was just too high – and why not send these discarded
volumes to people who might want or need them?

A pilot project in 2003 had thirty stores in the Pacific Northwest
sending the castoffs to the Fife warehouse where eight full-time scanners
scan their barcode numbers, grade the books for quality, and record them
with the huge Amazon Books online store. Those that Amazon wouldn't
accept because of minimum-price restrictions – or titles that were too
plentiful in Savers' stock – were either sent to an outside recycler for pulp-
ing or shipped by 50,000-pound container loads to India and Pakistan
("we produced 2 million pounds of export-quality material last year,"
Jonathan says).

The project was a success: while the Fife operation itself is so far at
break-even, the stores save about $90,000 a year in dumping costs. Now
the company has created its own store – saverstreasures – on the eBay
website half.com, where it sells books without barcodes and others that
are highly collectible, as well as CDs and videos (mostly fitness and children's titles and a surprising forty per cent without their original cases).
The plan is to greatly expand the eBay presence.

Among the treasures Jonathan has seen surfacing in the warehouse
is a coffee-table book reprinting the entire run of *The San Francisco
Oracle*, a newspaper published in the Haight-Ashbury area during the '60s

hippie era. Autographed by the journal's staff and inscribed to "Sam, the biggest Flying Brother," it sold for nearly $1,400. Jonathan felt personally responsible for trying to find the owner of a beautiful illustrated Bible that recorded a family's history from the 1840s to the 1960s. He failed, however, and the book sold for about $600. One story with a happier ending involved a book about Fred Astaire. Decades ago a New York woman had lost the book, inscribed to her, and had regretted its loss ever since. Looking on the Savers book site one day recently, she saw it described, right down to the inscription – and happily bought it back.

"Book recycling is definitely growing," John Lawless confirms. "And there's lots of opportunities for glass and other items. We have a waste stream that we're only scratching the surface of. My goal is that the only thing that goes into the garbage in a store is actual garbage – like a pizza box."

PASS ON THE SHOES

Mike Griffith – who tried to have John and Phil McMullen postpone their African trip after 9/11 – had long been a proponent of more recycling of Savers' discarded goods. "I convinced Tom to hire Phil on staff. He did a wonderful job of organizing that business and traveling and evangelizing about recycling in the company."

At one point Phil told him: "You've got to go to Africa with me."

"I was scared," Mike admits. "But I did go to India. He said it would be a life-changing experience for me. And it was."

In 2003 the two of them traveled to Ghandhidham, north of Bombay on the west coast of India, a major port and the country's only free-trade zone. Specially built for displaced persons after partition, it's a planned and relatively prosperous city. One of the aims of the trip was to videotape what Phil calls "a brilliant idea for a marketing campaign – to show a recycled pair of children's shoes and follow its path from its donation to the Savers sales floor to being ragged off, sent to the recycling plant and then to India to go on a little girl's feet."

Mike: "It's our last day. We have a Land Cruiser with a driver and to get out of Ghandhidham, you have to fly to a little airport to get to anoth-

Savers' own trucks help haul the mixed stew of goods that arrives for sorting and ship-ping in the two recycling centers in the U.S. and Canada.

er airport to get to Bombay." Driving into the ancient city of Bhuj, they stopped in a small squatters' village of cardboard-and-blanket shelters on the side of the road. Their local agent went looking for children to try on three kinds of footwear. After a succession of happy big and little kids in bare feet tried them on, a pair of white patent-leather shoes fit a girl of about six. Mike was recording the scene with video and still cameras. "I'm taking closeups and I notice all these people gathering around – maybe thirty or forty. I glance at the driver and he's looking concerned."

Marketing director Eric Farley had asked Phil and Mike to bring these special shoes back to the U.S. for the marketing campaign. The original idea was to give the kids' parents money to buy their own pairs. But Mike was getting very nervous. "We spot a group of young men across the street who don't look as happy as everyone else. And I tell Phil, 'Whoa! We're not taking the shoes off those kids.' We left the shoes."

It's no wonder that today Savers' recycling field managers always check to make sure that shoes suitable for recycling to the disadvantaged in nations like India haven't been tossed into trash barrels instead. And

Mike is pleased at the progress the company has made in the past decade. "At first, no one wanted recycling," he says. "I saw such great potential in it; so much good stuff got thrown away. It literally makes you cry when you see people who have nothing."

For newcomer Ken Alterman, Savers' recycling efforts were one crucial keystone of the corporate culture. Another, he would understand more deeply every day, was its inextricable link with prominent non-profit charities in three countries.

"Our association with Savers helps us support ever-more-critical research."

Caring Partners

CHAPTER TEN

Susan Guppy's team of seven men and women working at the Value Village in Burien, just south of Seattle, are a special group of people. The youngest is twenty-five, the oldest fifty. At any one time, a couple of them might be taking in goods from individual donors and offering receipts at an on-site donation center; another team member cleaning restrooms and emptying garbage bins; others in the production department breaking down cardboard boxes and putting clothes hangers on the assembly racks, or out on the sales floor sweeping, cleaning mirrors, collecting shopping carts, or tidying up the parking lot. They work five days a week, about five hours a day, with some of them commuting as far as twenty-five miles from either a family residence or a group home.

What distinguishes the seven is the fact that all are clients of the Northwest Center (NWC), the largest and most comprehensive service-provider for people with developmental disabilities in Washington state – and a partner with Savers Inc. Susan's role is habilitation (not *re*habilitation) supervisor: after her charges arrive in special public-access vans, she stays with her work team throughout the day. State funding pays for the project's support staff and administrative costs and about half the clients' wages. The company pays the rest.

The Burien store is the second-oldest in Washington; after a bad fire a few years ago, it was rebuilt and is now among the nicest (and most profitable) Villages in the Puget Sound area. And it's the only one in the state to be enhanced by the presence of a charity's supported work team.

Opposite: Canadian Diabetes' Clothesline trucks pick up donated household goods.

Northwest Center's supplying of an entire team to Savers began in 2002 when the store in Lake City, Washington, worked with the charity to fill an attendant position for a new donation station. The Center's client worked so well that he became a seasoned, full-time employee. After that success, the expanded project at Burien seemed a natural.

As well as hiring Susan's group, the store has another Northwest client, Martin Dullea, an individual employment placement who works on his own initiative. At thirty-eight, Martin was about to get married recently and obviously feeling good about life when he announced with a certain pride and confidence in his voice: "I am a man in love and I love my job! I work hard every day. I dust, mop, empty garbage, put down the mats, clean the break room. I just help out a lot. I work two hours a day and I take the bus to work in the morning. I love working with the people. It's a very good job."

On their website, the Northwest Center points out the mutual benefits of the Burien experience: "For the store, it's a necessary service that supports production staff who sift through huge inventories that must be moved quickly onto the floor, and for NWC it's an opportunity to give people with developmental disabilities a chance to receive vocational training in the community – a hallmark of the NWC's mission. Known for its large production facility or sheltered workshop, NWC wants instead to provide more work-training opportunities in natural business and retail settings through contracts such as these . . . .

"The NWC crew and Savers' staff are totally integrated and work side-by-side, occasionally performing the same tasks. Communication is outstanding; issues and concerns are brought directly to the crew and vice-versa. For the sake of the business, everything is taken seriously, but problems are handled with respect and understanding. The NWC supervisor and crew are kept abreast of Savers' company news, upcoming events, etc., while store staff and management are very interested in general aspects of vocational training programs, including program planning and residential services, and importantly, how they can help the crew become better workers.

"Over the years, the partnership helped fund NWC services, and now Savers itself provides successful employment and training opportunities for people with disabilities. However, we've learned recently that this

A client of the Northwest Center in Seattle is part of a special team that works under supervision in the Back Room at a Village in Burien, Washington.

is not an isolated occurrence; within their stores and production departments in other states, they're recreating their work environments to benefit workers with and without disabilities – as a result, Savers has been hiring more people with disabilities. [One example: in 1997 the store in Littleton, Colorado, hired two clients of United Cerebral Palsy of Colorado as job-sharing jewelry pricers. One of the women was in a wheelchair, the other was mute and had limited mobility; both could do the job.] Savers is not simply a growing company of thrift department stores, but a company with a human-services mission. Kudos to Savers!"

On the other side of the country, Kimberly Weir and Alycia Solivan of Springfield, Massachusetts, share a special bond. Kimberly has a master's degree in human services, focusing on organizational management and leadership. For the past sixteen years she has worked for the Connecticut Department of Corrections, starting as a corrections officer. Now a major – a step below a warden – she helps rehabilitate the male inmates of an intermediate-level prison and prepare them to return to the community. Kim is also a single mother of a twenty-one-year-old daughter attending college. Alycia is a sweet, enthusiastic twelve-year-old with a working

Supporting children who need adult role models, Big Brothers Big Sisters organizations across North America value their financial links with Savers.

mother, a grandmother who helps at home, a brother, and two sisters. Well, *three* sisters: for the past five years Kim Weir has been her Big Sister, a volunteer mentor offering her Little Sister one-on-one advice and support.

The pair are part of Big Brothers Big Sisters (BBBS), the largest mentoring organization in the U.S., serving more than 200,000 children, aged six through eighteen, in five thousand communities in every state. Regional organizations from Long Island, New York, to Maui, Hawaii, have partnered with Savers in a mutually beneficial relationship. (The company has similar alliances with many of the organization's 170 agencies across Canada.) The proceeds from the donated goods BBBS delivers to the thrift stores fund a non-profit charity that achieves tangible successes: about half the Little Brothers and Little Sisters are less likely to skip school or start using illegal drugs than their peers and more than a quarter of them are less likely to start using alcohol.

On a personal basis, Kim finds huge emotional paybacks in her relationship with Alycia. "When I first joined, they required that you spend at least six hours a month with a child. Alycia and I can spend six hours together in one day! She loves going to an ice-cream restaurant here, a dinner there. Sometimes she wants to do that and a movie too. Sometimes we just go to the mall and hang out or she comes over to my house and we bake cookies. My Little often goes to church with me, whenever she's not singing in her choir. I know Alycia gets a chance to do a lot of things with me that she probably wouldn't get to do at home because her mother has other children" – who have also had Big Sisters or Big Brothers.

Alycia could be quoting Kim when she describes their days together: "We go to the mall, we go to restaurants, we eat ice cream, we hang out. Kim is great. We have lots of fun. I love it! Everyone should have a Big Sister."

Kim: "It is just an awesome way to give back to your community. To help other children and to introduce them to things that are positive. To be a positive role model in their life. My daughter loves having Alycia around, and she's looking into becoming a Big as well. "

Up north in Canada, Bob Teskey is a special poster boy for the Canadian Diabetes Association. He's hardly a boy, of course: at fifty-nine, the Edmonton lawyer is the well-seasoned and very living proof that CDA funding is helping to make an enormous difference in the lives of diabetics – not only in the True North Strong and Free but in the rest of the world, too. Bob was diagnosed with diabetes at age fourteen, but about a decade ago he started blacking out because of low blood sugar, and the severe injuries he suffered in an automobile accident were taking years to heal. After hearing about a possible new treatment at the University of Alberta, he became one of the first patients with Type 1 diabetes to enrol in a revolutionary experiment being run by researchers in the Clinical Islet Laboratory.

Dr. Jonathan Lakey was the lab director overseeing the test of a new form of islet transplantation, a fifteen-minute operation to introduce sound insulin-producing cells from human pancreases into the livers of diabetics. He and his colleagues, including the pioneering Dr. Ray Rajotte of Alberta and the current leader, Dr. James Shapiro of England, have treated seventy-four patients in Canada. Worldwide, about 500 have undergone the procedure. The Edmonton Protocol – named for the university's home city – is not yet a permanent cure, but it's more successful than anything else devised so far. About eighty per cent of those with transplants have been off their daily insulin injections for at least one year, half for more than three years. While Bob Teskey had to resume his after four years, he says the disease is much more manageable because his transplanted cells are still generating insulin.

The Globe and Mail, a national Canadian newspaper, recently called the protocol "a medical breakthrough so historic and extraordinary that it has been hailed as the most important development in diabetes research since Canadian doctors introduced insulin to the world in 1922, a feat that earned them the Nobel Prize." Bob Teskey simply calls it "a personal miracle."

Even more diabetics could have been treated by now if not for the sobering fact that the procedure depends on the donations of organs from people who are clinically brain-dead and who may be in hospitals anywhere in Canada ("I'm on call twenty-four a day, seven days a week," Dr. Lakey said at one point). The lab team's work also depends on funding from governments and community sources – among them the Canadian Diabetes Association, which over the years has played a small yet significant part in financially backing the protocol researchers.

And the CDA, in turn, has been dependent to a large degree on the key business liaison it has with Value Village stores across Canada, supplying forty-five per cent of their volume and over the years earning an estimated $200 million in the bargain. As Glenn Manderson, now the organization's VP of business operations, points out, "The work that we've done in our association with Savers has allowed us to support ever-more-critical research – and one of the key successes in recent years is the Edmonton Protocol."

BUSINESS WITH A HEART

Since those long-ago days when Bill Ellison started collaborating with groups assisting veterans of World War II, the profitable company that became Savers has paid well over $1 billion to registered non-profit charities in the United States, Canada, and Australia. And both parties to this reciprocal back-scratching arrangement never forget that their success relies entirely on the largesse of the public, who are the heart of the business.

What prompts people to donate their castoff clothing and household effects to non-profit charities? In the United States one of the more pragmatic reasons may simply be to get a bit of a tax break. The Internal Revenue Service allows donors to deduct the "fair market value" – the price a willing buyer would pay – for items donated to qualified charities. Most folks guess at the value, although entrepreneurs have leaped in to help. One company produced a booklet called *Ca$h for Your Used Clothing*, which evaluates about 750 items based on annual surveys of thrift stores and consignment shops, while a computer-software group offers a program called ItsDeductible, listing 10,000 items. The IRS even allows taxpayers driving to drop off their goods at a charity to claim a deduction of fourteen cents a mile. But it recently imposed new rules on those who request deductions of $500 or more for donating vehicles to non-profits (as many as 730,000 people a year make such claims). The regulations now limit the deduction to the sale price received by a charity for a vehicle, although there are special circumstances where the donor may claim fair market value. This change might be the thin edge of a mighty wedge: in 2005 some U.S. senators were studying the possibility of reducing or eliminating tax breaks for all non-cash charitable donations.

In the end, even if the tax relief disappears, there's a good chance the donations will continue at almost the same level. Canada has never offered such breaks to donors and the charities there have exceptionally strong donation programs. Besides, householders will always need someplace to absorb their unwanted goods, and giving them to a non-profit rather than tossing them in the trash should appeal to most people's consciences.

The first Partners Advisory Board: (Back row, left to right) Gordon Therriault, Big Brothers Big Sisters; Gary White; Buddy Grimmett; David Cooper, Association for Retarded Citizens of Clark County; Dennis McGill; June Mansfield, Community Services for the Blind and Partially Sighted. (Front row) Glenn Manderson, Canadian Diabetes; Ellen Spiess; Linda Searfoss, Big Brothers Big Sisters; Tom Beaton (Savers board consultant); Jean Kantu, Northwest Center.

At least, that's the hope of the dedicated men and women who run the charities that deal with Savers. "People are usually grateful for the service; it tangibly helps the community and helps clean your closets," says David Cooper, the burly, bewhiskered executive director of The Arc of Clark County, based in Vancouver, Washington. Arc is an advocate for the rights of people with development disabilities and their families. For a decade David was a socially conscious Democratic legislator in the House of Representatives and for the past dozen years has been with Arc, increasing its budget seven-fold to more than $2.2 million with Savers' help. Its many programs include guardianship of more than forty people, with eighty-five per cent of the funds flowing from the donated goods it sells to the company.

"Part of the dilemma with non-profits," David says, "is that the executives hire on to help people, but the notion of the 'business' needed to generate funds is a whole extra step that's uncomfortable for some of them. I view it as almost the polar opposite: it's beholden on us to raise as much funding as possible to support our mission. Unfortunately, a lot of non-profits see this as something you have to do to do the other thing.... What I wanted from Savers was a fair price and an opportunity. This isn't rocket science. It is hard work. Every day you turn the light on, you've got to earn your keep; there's no coasting."

David Cooper is a member of Savers' Partners Advisory Board – key leaders of charitable organizations the company consults about issues that inevitably arise in the relationship between non-profits and a for-profit enterprise. The board meets quarterly in various North American cities and there's an annual Partners Conference, which the advisors help organize, to which all the charities are invited. Despite their criticism – about inefficient truck-unloading facilities, the failure to accept certain merchandise, the price paid for each OK – the non-profit partners readily acknowledge the rich value of the company's expertise. "We could no more efficiently and profitably run a thrift store than I could run to the moon," David says. "They pay us a fair price – more than Goodwill, which has approached me. Tom and his family have really been generous, when it has not been in Savers' best interest."

Bill Tymann, the silver-bearded CEO of Big Brothers Big Sisters of Long Island has had similar experience with the company. A sociology grad of Fordham University, he began his career as a case worker with the Little Flower Children's Service in Brooklyn and rose to assistant director. In 1997 he joined a small, struggling BBBS agency in Nassau County as executive director and through creative entrepreneurship funded a budget that grew to $1.2 million a year. Working with Savers was a crucial element in his game plan. "I got them into Long Island before they opened any stores there. I'm rather persistent," he says. "And for a year or two, they held our hand, taught us the business. They gave us a startup grant of $100,000 and loaned us another $17,000 to get us going."

His organization was drawing on the used clothing and merchandise of three million well-off people in two counties. "We started with four leased trucks and one shift of [phone-solicitation] diallers. We learned three things very quickly: One, we needed to continue to learn. Two, we didn't have the competition that other charities have across the country. Goodwill, St. Vincent de Paul, and the Salvation Army were long-established there and the business was so lucrative that they weren't very innovative in their methodologies. None of them were using telemarketers. And thirdly, the quality of clothing was the best that Savers had seen in North America." It was so good that the company began shipping it across the continent to supply other outlets. Only after two years did Savers open the first of its two stores on Long Island.

But the relationship soon hit a rough patch. By late 1999 there was so much good product available that it was glutting the market. The company had to drastically cut the supply from the agency – at the same time that the Nassau County government reneged on a large grant to the local BBBS. After laying off staff, Bill Tymann had to regroup. He asked Tom and Buddy Grimmett, then in charge of vendor relations, to release him from the contract provision that promised exclusivity of supply to the company. Bill also wanted to sell to private brokers of used goods in the credentials market. "And Savers said Yes. There was a time there over a year where our contract was a verbal one from month to month." Eventually, as the company itself regrouped, it was able to absorb the Long Island supply stream again and Bill was able to pull back from the ruthlessly run credentials world.

The experience had shown him how unique the people of Savers were. "They really did care about the charities, even when they messed up. When I learned the business, I learned there's no one else like them out there. They really believe they're helping the local community. And that's the essence of the Ellisons."

Both Tom Ellison and Ken Alterman believe that Savers is, and must be, hand in glove with the charities that fill its stores with all those everyday good buys and the occasional treasures. Their mindset is reflected in the fact that the company always prefers to call the non-profits their partners – just as it refers to employees as team members. They signaled their continuing respect for this relationship not long ago, at a Partners Advisory Board meeting in Vancouver. The spirited and often critical talk had been about how unprepared some of the stores were to handle the charities' truckloads of donations.

"We're still too top-bound," Tom admitted at one point. "We have to encourage all our people to work together to make decisions at the lowest possible level."

Ken agreed: "The process is broken.... We have to fix the system that affects your operations and the stores'."

Tom assured the participants: "This business was started on the basis that the charity's always right – almost. It sounds like I'm talking roses, but I believe it can be the case."

"It's really all about communication, education," Ken summed up. "And if it works for you, it works for us."

By meeting's end, the partners were pleased at the company's level of understanding of their problems. "The tone and productivity in this meeting is a benchmark that hasn't been achieved before," said Keith Powell, executive director of Community Living Ontario, serving people with intellectual disabilities. "It starts to feel like a team."

Bill Tymann seemed to summarize the feeling in the room when he said, with a lot of heads nodding in agreement, "We deal with a lot of companies – and no company comes close to the care and core values you folks have."

Early on in his new role as VP and general manager, Ken had realized that truth for himself as he hit the ground running. Or, rather, walking around.

"Ken is willing to stop the analysis and make a decision."

FIFTY YEARS ON

CHAPTER ELEVEN

As the company approached its fiftieth year, one of every 125 Americans was a millionaire. Vodafone had just introduced Japan's first cellphone with a tiny embedded TV tuner. Movie theaters were featuring *Kill Bill* and *The Return of the King*. Elvis had died in Memphis a quarter-century ago, but his legend still lived on. In Alberta the $1-billion West Edmonton Mall, the world's largest shopping center, was soon to be eclipsed by a $1.3-billion mall in China. And in Bellevue, Washington, Savers had a new hand at the helm to guide it through the shoals of the early twenty-first century. Total revenues for 2003: more than $400 million.

What impressed many people about Ken Alterman's first weeks with Savers was the fact that he didn't leap in and make independent judgments like his predecessor, Gary White. In fact, he employed that most basic of communication tactics, management by walking around – and observing and listening. "Two days after he arrived," Ellen Spiess notes, "he began to spend the next three weeks out in the stores, not in his office. He worked in the Redmond store for four days and then in a Canadian store for a week." He was even found in the Back Rooms, sorting clothes, *very slowly*. "It was just so important for Tom that Ken understood the business. He's a very friendly guy; he'll talk to anybody. He's direct but very personable and can relate to store managers in a genuine way."

Buddy Grimmett, snugly back in the loss-prevention field, had a similar take on his new boss: "Gary came in with a bull-in-the-china-shop approach. Ken has come in with a more analytical, let's-learn-about-the-

Opposite: CEO Ken Alterman has brought a fresh professionalism to Savers.

culture of the organization. Overall, Ken sees a huge upside in Savers and it seems so simple to him compared to other businesses or manufacturing operations. It's going to be interesting. We're still a transitional company. We want to remain this family-type culture, but growth demands some change. We're a resilient business and we can overcome – I hope it doesn't take us forever to figure things out. We've got to get back on the growth machine and allow people the same opportunity I saw when I joined this company."

The national director of business operations of Canadian Diabetes – the charity most intimately linked with Savers – welcomed Ken's arrival on the scene. "Tom has found an extremely good guy in Ken and I hope he can keep him," Glenn Manderson said. "He was brought on to run a business, but it is a business that has to deal, on a day-to-day basis, with charities" – and many of the larger non-profits are bringing big-business skills into play, operating in some cases like Fortune 500 companies. "So it's a crucial step getting someone like Ken who can see both sides of that equation."

BATTING IN THE RUNS

Over his first two years Ken was keenly observing the strengths and flaws in the operation. Wandering through the Back Rooms and sales floors, he spotted seemingly small lapses that had large implications. Careless handling of clothing, for instance: "Generally what happens is that over the course of the day, stores get shopped pretty hard and there's a lot of stuff off hangers and in dressing rooms. Anything by a dressing room is really important because someone made a selection and recognized that this was a nice item. I've been to a ton of stores where, because we run out of time, a lot of that product goes right to the back into a recycle bin. That's one of the worst things we can do with that; it doesn't get put back into inventory. Then you go through a rack and see things that don't belong there – youth in ladies' or men's in ladies' – or merchandise that's the wrong size in the wrong place. That's dead inventory; it has no chance of selling. There's many examples of not managing that floor properly, not valuing the inventory like it's money."

He also came to realize that there could be a sizable increase in earnings if team members could identify just one more good, salable item in each OK from a charity and then get it on to the floor. Out of each bag, averaging thirty to forty items of clothing, some stores might get as few as fifteen usable pieces, others as many as twenty. If Savers receives fourteen million OKs a year and sells just one more piece of clothing out of every OK, at an average of $3.50, it would generate nearly $50 million more a year. "And that drops right down to the bottom line because it doesn't cost us anything extra to sell one more item," he points out. "That would double the company's profitability."

Ken's observations began to spark internal discussions about the amount and quality of merchandise that makes it on to the sales floors. One viewpoint was held by Shannon, who'd recently made two life-transforming moves: she got married and was now Shannon Vernerey and she'd been asked to relocate across the border to the Bellevue headquarters and become vice-president of global operations. Her mantra had long been: *Get as much product out there as possible.* "On the U.S. side," she says, "we were not processing enough merchandise. Canada has always processed a ton more than the U.S. As we increased product, that led to more sales. The more we get, the more 'treasures' there are."

In a real sense, she's right: the more selection, the better. But that concept can backfire if the racks are so jammed with product that customers have a hard time wading through it. So being selective about the merchandise is important, Ken argues. "It's not how many pieces you put out on the floor, we have to get smarter about what percentage of them we sell. If in fact you're running at thirty per cent and another store is at fifty per cent, one reason is probably sheer customer count. But number two is that you're putting out a lot of unsalable merchandise. So how do I identify you as someone who's putting out items that are not salable? Or that you have a product-supply issue in that you're not getting good stuff? The measurements we use now are not action-oriented enough. Part of the problem is just talent, some is our reporting system.

"It comes down to understanding what's happening in your store. Not anecdotally, which is what this company has been built on, but really by measuring it – knowing what percentage of your sales is ladies' tops, for example. We don't know yet where we make our money. And the

Phil Davis (right) headed the Retail Initiatives Group, which includes Eric Farley (left), Buddy Grimmett (middle), Mike Bacon, and David Weiss.

way to measure that is to break your business down. So we've created a new group here called our Retail Business Initiative, RBI [in Ken's favorite sport, baseball, that abbreviation means "runs batted in"]. To really grow you need to have a group whose sole focus is working one or two of these levers in the business."

Until recently, the RBI group was headed by newcomer Phil Davis, vice-president of retail business initiatives. The economics grad of Stanford University (where he and his wife both knew Lea Anne Ottinger) had worked in the corporate-lending field in Manhattan, helped run the family electrical-distribution business for eleven years, and later became operations VP in charge of distributing upscale garments for Cutter & Buck of Seattle. More recently he'd created his own website for artists and craftspeople to sell their work online and was the executive VP of operations for a startup website, housevalues.com, that became very profitable within six months and then went public. That online business to generate real-estate leads intrigued Ken: "It's a pretty innovative concept. After it provides you an appraisal of your house for free, the information from your request goes to nearby realtors who pay for the service and then they call you."

Phil had been looking for a new challenge when he networked with both Lea Anne and John Meisenbach about Savers. Ken and Tom first interviewed him to run the sourcing department – to succeed Scott Blomquist, who'd moved to Utah and, uncertain about his future with the company, had reluctantly left after more than two decades of dedicated service.

But Phil wasn't lured by that job and waited until being offered a chance to rescue a point-of-sale project to replace the stores' old electronic cash registers with PC-based ones. It wasn't worth rescuing, he determined, and with a new information-technology director he'd known at Cutter & Buck – John Leitch – Phil launched a different two-year project. "It wasn't really a cash-register issue," he says. "The problem we were trying to solve is the ability to collect information about what we're selling, when we're selling, and at what price – so we can make better decisions about what we're producing in the Back Room and how we're selling it in the store."

Ken, impressed by Phil's reasoning, put him in charge of the new RBI group, which includes four company stalwarts. As Phil described their roles:

"Mike Bacon is vice-president of store initiatives. He's a valuable linkage to the past and has a very keen understanding of the business model and store operations. He's able to build rapport with the store folk" – and tactfully lead initiatives in the pre-deployment phase of any project.

"Eric Farley, as marketing director, has a lot of history too. Over the years, marketing has had inconsistent support. Tom's not a great believer in it, while Ken is." While some people say that the important goal is to get more OKs into the system, Phil and Eric argue for effective brand-building and media coverage, among other things. "Eric has been a very vocal proponent of those and sometimes has to go into stealth mode to get them done.

"Buddy Grimmett runs Loss Prevention, which really represents a group that can help us execute our best practices. The greatest loss we have as a company is either the loss of employees or the opportunity to even attract quality employees.

"David Weiss, manager of new store development, has been here for several years and it's amazing how fast he is at connecting the dots and interpreting what's going on. [Ken says David "can put together an Excel spreadsheet faster than anybody I've ever seen in my life."] We've had such a horrible track record in new-store openings in the U.S. in the last five to ten years. He'll help ensure we take the proper steps to make a good site selection and execute a successful opening – and still *own* that store afterward until it's become profitable." In two successive weeks in mid-2005, stores in Reno and Rochester, Minnesota, broke the American three-day grand-opening sales records.

In keeping with Ken's step-by-step approach to innovation, RBI launched three tests of new practices in a sampling of stores around Savers' world. One is to simplify pricing. Currently clothing pricers, for example, have so many options ranging between one and ten dollars that it's hard to make fine distinctions about what a garment might be worth. "And a customer looks at different jeans at $2, $3, and $4 and asks, 'Why?'" Phil said. "Who knows? It's an art form. So we have a high turn-over in our Back Rooms, constantly training new pricers." The test was to remove some price points to create a greater spread between the pricing options. The danger, of course, was that customers might like having many different prices; the test would help determine whether that's true.

A second experiment was to ticket products with barcodes on sticky labels that identify exactly what a particular item is, what size, and how much it costs. This is all done in an instant at a fixed pricing station with a touch-screen interface. A scanner then captures all this data to give an accurate reading of what's selling in that store. "This will let us see if people are doing an effective job on a local level," he said at the time. "They can prove that their customers do buy cups without saucers, for instance. I'm hoping this information will continue to empower the stores to make their own decisions locally."

And the third test involved controlling the flow of goods to the stores. Savers' stores weren't making maximum use of the goods that individuals brought them as on-site donations (OSDs) and that cost the company less than the goods the charities have to pick up. "This is the one that presents us with the greatest opportunity for huge profitability," said Phil. "Instead of having non-profits delivering a certain amount of product to your store every day, we'll have a filter called a flow-control center. The charity delivers to a central depot and the product is held there while

Stores branded with the name "Savers" through much of the U.S. and in Melbourne, Australia, attract young families, among other shrewd shoppers.

the store goes after OSDs. Then the store calls the flow-control center and says how much merchandise it needs tomorrow [to supplement the OSD stream]. Maximizing OSDs in a market benefits us because of the lower cost of goods and also benefits the charities because they don't have to do anything to profit from this." And the non-profits save time by delivering donations to a single center, rather than having their trucks waiting to unload at slow receiving stations in the stores.

In July 2005 Phil left Savers to pursue a philanthropic passion: to run the Hoh River Trust, a not-for-profit organization that owns and manages land in Washington state's Hoh River Valley for the benefit of fish, wildlife, and people. "Phil's greatest strength," Ken says, "was making people get comfortable with change. He had a very disarming way of introducing new ideas to achieve team-member alignment."

Ken had already put into practice a new tool called SPAM, for Store Planning Action Model. Among other things, SPAM compares an individual store's pricing against the company's equivalent outlets in its district. For example, a store might be setting an average price per ladies' garment of $5.44 while the district average is $6.12. Perhaps that store is pricing the low end of the product too high – charging $3.99 instead of, say, $1.99 – and thus discouraging shoppers from buying. By being more analytical, managers might identify price points that are lacking in their stores. "Right now the SPAM reports are in the hands of regional and district managers," he says. "It's an action tool for them to prioritize where they need to spend their time as they're helping store by store."

Through initiatives like this, Ken Alterman has infused the former family enterprise with a more professional and sophisticated big-business approach – all the while trying to preserve the small-company values the Ellisons embraced from the beginning. "Ken and I aren't that dissimilar, personality-wise, and we like the same things," Tom points out. "Our backgrounds and the way that we execute are different. I am much more of a seat-of-the-pants decision-maker. He can analyze better, but he's not analytical to a fault. He is willing to stop the analysis and make a decision. One of the best compliments I could pay Ken is that he sees things that need to get done, but he's patient about it – because he understands that here is this unique and long-standing culture and we value people that have been around for a long time."

In early 2005 Tom and the board named Ken president and CEO of Savers. The challenge will be, as it is for all quickly growing companies, to preserve the original, Ellison-inspired corporate culture in the face of widespread dispersion and continuing crops of new employees.

FRESH FACES

Among the head-office people Ken hired is Jon Kroon, vice-president of business partnerships and logistics – a fancier title for sourcing, or liaising with the charities about product supply. Jon, a young-looking Chicagoan in his early fifties, had an ecelctic background that includes about two years with Levi Strauss, where he became the jeans-maker's internal-audit director and did special projects for the board of directors; and six years with Target Stores, where he got to know Gary White and became the number-two executive of a distribution center he opened and expanded in Sacramento and then doubled the size of a facility in Pueblo, Colorado. He spent a briefer time as VP of logistics at West Marine of Santa Cruz, California, the large national boating-supplies chain; and most recently (and surprisingly) as senior vice-president of operations at the troubled Frederick's of Hollywood, famous for its bras, panties, lingerie, and sexy women's apparel.

"I've always wanted to be with a business that makes a difference," Jon explains about his move to Savers. "What pushed me into taking the position was the people here. People with longevity and their talk of values instead of treating people like forklifts." He realized that Buddy, when he'd become responsible again for sourcing, had an almost-impossible job of dealing with eighty charity partners in 120 offices. Jon arrived at a time when the department was being restructured to add seven partner-relations managers who team up with the stores' regional managers to oversee product supply; it has since also named a manager of inventory control and supply-chain management.

On the job he was soon excited about bringing in charities such as the all-volunteer Bosom Buddies in Phoenix, which helps women get mammograms in mobile test stations, and Children's Advocacy Centers in Tucson and Denver, which provide a safe environment for abused kids. "Funding to keep groups like this going is what makes this business so different."

New trends under his watch include signing contracts with the non-profits for three years instead of two and guaranteeing that Savers will buy a certain number of OKs per week rather than guaranteeing that the partners will make a profit. As a result, two Big Brothers Big Sisters in the U.S. have ended their relationship with the company (while in Canada a BBBS in Winnipeg began one). "People think it's easy money," Jon says of the charities' donation-supply business. "But if you really have to make it profitable, it's *serious* business. Those partners that do well hire professional operations people. That's why the Canadian Diabetes Association is so successful."

The aggressive CDA had long wanted to partner with its sister organization, American Diabetes Association, to create a Diabetes North America that would collect donations in the U.S. and sell them to thrift stores. During Gary White's tenure, the CDA's Glenn Manderson made a spirited effort to get the two charities together to launch a pilot operation in Detroit, but the U.S. group wasn't keen. Finally, in 2005 the CDA and the ADA signed a letter of agreement that would have the Canadians offer

Anne Dessi and Dave Allgood in the human-resources department make sure that fun – even in workshops – is a key part of the company's retreats.

technical expertise to the Americans, who would gather goods in their own name and ideally supply Savers. The first such arrangement, expected to start in Denver, could herald a major breakthrough for the company in the U.S. market.

When Ken Alterman arrived, two recent newcomers to the human-resources department in the U.S. were already in place, hired by Gary: Anne Dessi and Dave Allgood. Anne, with a sociology degree from Western Washington University, had been a training specialist with the Red Robin International restaurant chain and then a VP of human resources for both the audio giant Harman International and Starbucks in Seattle during its great growth spurt. When she joined Savers in 2000 at age forty, her mandate was to build a HR organization to drive growth – "to run key training programs, put best practices out there, and start succession planning [for the stores, districts, and regions]." She also oversees payroll, compensation, and benefits: "Our store managers earn ninety-five per cent of the market rate and, with bonus compensation, they're way over the top. It's not uncommon for them to make $50,000 to $80,000 a year."

One of her department's major vehicles has been a workshop to develop high-potential successors – LEAD, for Leadership Experience and Development – which brings up to twenty people to head office for four days. Two outside consultants and staff people coach and assess the candidates one-on-one as they take personality tests and do situational-leadership exercises, leading them to create their own career growth plan. They learn the company's five core values, the first of which is that "team members are the source of our success." As Anne says, "In the past we've lost a lot of great people. If we don't get them into training right away, they don't feel connected or know what the core values are."

Dave Allgood came to work with Anne in 2002 as training director. Although his master's degree was in English, the forty-eight-year-old wound up as a training manager for the software company Egghead and AT&T Wireless and as a consultant in management development for major companies such as the Chapters book chain in Canada. Scott Blomquist had already asked him consult to Savers in 1997 to develop JumpStart. The CD-based program in English, French, or Spanish allows newcomers to work through five modules, on their own and with the counsel of store managers, to learn the key corporate facts and philosophy. "The idea," he says, "is that there's more to this company than just the little store they're working in, so they feel they're part of a bigger entity."

Dave now trains people to confront performance problems, using a videotape that features interviews with fellow employees, and is revising a bulky guide for trainers of store managers – "all these lessons need to be revisited and made more experiential" and possibly put on a website so they can be more self-directed like the JumpStart program.

He and Anne organize large-group training at the managers' and supervisors' retreats that are so rooted in the company's culture. A retreat planning team brings together marketing, operations, travel coordination, and HR to create entertaining, informative modules of business strategy, communication, training and education, and celebrating success. As Dave says, "Incorporating fun into these retreats is paramount, even in the workshops. Gone are the days of monotonous speeches and transparencies – retreat attendees are treated to interactive seminars with funny movie vignettes, role-playing, motivational speakers, and engaging graphic presentations. And we choose the workshops to address top requests identified by a survey of store and district managers long before the event." The settings help: a beachfront hotel in Maui, for instance, or Universal City, California, where employees can enjoy the attractions of Universal Studios.

With Gary's departure, Dave had worried about how large a role training would play after the transition to a new corporate leader. "I knew Anne got the value of training. But I was kind of sweating it when Gary left. Fortunately, Ken seldom gives a company address when he doesn't mention the importance of training people well."

Ken's cast of mind has also proved a boon for Gina Cohen, who arrived in 2002 as a communications specialist. A native of Seattle, she'd been an associate publisher and spokeswoman for a Nashville bridal magazine and a marketing-communications manager for a medical software firm. "On my first day on the job, our Langley store caught fire and the B.C. press was calling about how team members rescued somebody," Gina recalls. "And Gary White had just left and I had to talk to Tom about why. I could feel the tension. It felt a little quicksandy that first week." Ken succeeded Gary a few months later and, coming from the media-savvy Pepsico, supported her initiatives.

She visited all the district managers and with a public-relations firm put together media kits and key messaging documents with frequently asked questions. "Nobody had ever done media training for managers and the executive team." She also revitalized a lackluster website and created an e-mail newsletter for customers that now has 30,000 subscribers. Her most innovative ploy was choreographing the Savers Showroom! display in Manhattan. "The national magazine media didn't know us. So what better way than just to show up and be in their face?" The expense of outfitting the showroom and hosting the editors seemed more than justified when some of the top young women's magazines responded enthusiastically in print to the company's informal and funky style. Wendy Wallace, fashion market editor for *Marie Claire*, commented on-site, "This is incredible. I feel like it's my birthday. We do an under-$100 column and usually feature K-Mart and Target, but these projects are more fun!"

CATCHING UP WITH THE CAST

Gina Cohen was collaborating with veterans Eric Farley and Becky Henchman, who were bringing fresh levels of innovation to the Savers brand. "We're embarking on a new process – the leadership has changed a lot and the business has changed a little," Eric concedes. "We need to update the stores with a brand that deals with selling, accepting donations, and recycling. And we need to compete: there are fantastic thrift stores out there that do a bang-up job and this gets more intensive every year." He and Ken hired a brand-design firm to do focus groups and market research to re-identify the customer base. (An in-house report to set the stage for such a study described the Savers shopper as "frugal by nature, feels 'used' is smarter, will spend time and be excited by the opportunity to save money, and appreciates a sense of control and the 'thrill of the hunt'.")

Eric sees three challenges ahead: "One is just making the shopping experience even better. In the visual presentation inside the store, we're certainly a guiding force with better signage that's more intuitive [for the customer to comprehend]." But he feels there's more work to do in floor layout and merchandise display.

"Then there are some challenges with the different names of the company. Corporately we're all Savers now. And it's hard to imagine us changing the name Value Village in Canada – it's the least-considered option up there. But operating as Value Village in the U.S. outside of the Pacific Northwest has become a challenge because the name has slipped into the public domain." Although one idea has been to rebrand as "Savers Value Village," no quick and easy solution has yet presented itself.

And the third problem is how to balance the force of the Halloween season with the rest of the year: "The nature of that beast occupies two months. It displaces a lot of used merchandise and brings the challenge of new merchandise – opening boxes and putting it on shelves – and then it goes away again. We have to do a better job of moving in and out of the season and exposing those customers coming in for Halloween to the rest of our stores."

His department has helped attract the costume-seekers with a recent intriguing commercial. For four years the company had called their annual autumn event the Halloween Factory. And in 2004 a TV spot capitalized on the name by being shot in an enormous electrical-generating plant built for cable cars in the Seattle of the early 1900s. More than fifty employees and their families gathered late at night in what's now an atmospheric museum to became ghosts and ghouls under the mad eye of the green-haired Dr. Frankenfrugal.

Savers' great and growing success with All Hallow's Eve has also resulted from Becky's initiative. In 2001, not long after Eric convinced her to come back to the company, she prepared a game plan for the Halloween Factory. She headed a team that included Eric, Scott, Shannon, Mike Bacon, and Mike Davison – the Canadian district manager who'd been pushing people for years to get serious about the season. "It's the single thing I'm most proud of," Becky says. In six weeks she developed a plan for merchandising, promoting, and advertising – and then training staff at a Halloween Summit for store managers in Albuquerque in place of the annual retreat. A seventy-eight-page briefing book went out to all stores, with a week-by-week schedule detailing everything from how to receive the seasonal merchandise to what to say in public-address announcements ("Here's a scary thought! Halloween is just around the corner and you have no idea what you're going to be!") The hard work of employees wasn't ignored: the document suggested free staff lunches on October Fridays, prizes for team-member costumes, and four big winners for designing the best "Moonlight Madness" in-store party for customers.

"Before then, we had big Halloweens," Becky reports. "But since then we've had record-breaking September-to-Octobers now that we're doing it globally as a consistent brand through the stores. We want to *own* the holiday."

The irony is that Mike Davison, the long-time district manager who had been promoting Halloween for fifteen years, is no longer with Savers. Feeling a bit unappreciated, he left in 2005 after twenty years to set up his own business. Yet the outspoken Canadian continued to speak well of both Tom and Ken: "I have a lot of respect for Value Village. For the business model and mostly for Tom Ellison, his leadership, as a mentor – everything." And the last time he met Ken, Mike said, "I really like you and I like the way your mind works – as long as you're prepared to walk

In 2001 a creative new merchandising, promotional, and advertising game plan helped turn Savers into the Halloween Superstore across North America.

the talk. You know, when Tom lets you play your role as president, you'll make a good one." He told Tom the same thing and, as he later recalled, "The next time Tom phoned me, he said, 'By the way, you know Ken is now the president.'"

Shannon Vernerey, meanwhile, is no longer vice-president of global operations. Ken asked her to focus again on Canada as VP of Canadian operations. The new VP of U.S. operations is Chad Buscho, who had been a regional vice-president in charge of 131 oulets for Jo-Anne Stores Inc., the largest retailer serving the U.S. craft and fabric industry. Earlier he had been director of custom framing at Michaels Stores, the arts and crafts chain, and fashions manager at K-Mart Corporation.

As Ken explained in a memo to staff, "It has become increasingly apparent that our businesses in Canada and the U.S. have different challenges that require 100 per cent of each leader's time.... The retail landscape in Canada has changed quite a bit the last few years with stronger competition and a more challenging labor market to contend with. Because of her familiarity with all aspects of Value Village Stores, Shannon is the logical choice to lead and bolster this critical business unit for us." There was urgency to the move: the previous year was the first that Canada hadn't reached its quotas, and Canadian stores can represent as much as three-quarters of the company's profits. Wal-Mart and Winners were encroaching on Value Village, more American retailers were entering the large Quebec market, and there were rumors of Target Stores coming north of the border.

Jeff Smail was moved back to Vancouver as western director of Canadian operations, reporting to Shannon – who would remain in Bellevue, so she, Ken, and Chad Buscho could work closely together. "Having a professional of Shannon's experience," Ken wrote, "gives our company the confidence that our vital Canadian business will be strong so that our accelerator on growth does not slow down."

Shannon would again be working in tandem with Brenda Seraphim, the Canadian HR director, who was increasingly concentrating on labor relations. Unions in the U.S. have made little inroads on Savers – although an attempt to organize a store a few years ago in East Providence, Rhode Island, was narrowly voted down – but labor organizers have had slightly more success in Canada. Yet as of this writing there were no unions in place across the country. Brenda and key store managers have managed to defuse potential employee revolts and even create the right workplace climate to reverse union certifications.

A good example is the Value Village in Whitby, Ontario, near the strong labor town of Oshawa, where the Canadian Auto Workers is the predominant union. "The CAW didn't come looking for us," Brenda explains. "Our team members went looking for them because those people were not managed properly. And the shame of it was that we were taking action against the manager but just didn't take it fast enough. Then Pete Bellis was transferred into the store as manager and he persevered over four years and kept our core values. He is tough, charming, and charismatic and has taken every opportunity to show that the team members are not well served by paying somebody else a fee to represent their interest. If it were not for Pete, none of this would have happened. It's all about relationships."

The atmosphere at the store improved so much that employees began organizing a decertification drive. In January 2005, after three applications to decertify, employees led by cashier Anne Millward finally succeeded in going non-union again.

A different situation arose in Prince George, B.C., when Brenda Beecroft – now the district manager in Greater Vancouver as well as Prince George – opened the location and from the start put it into the top ten among Villages across Canada. "What happened in Prince George probably hasn't happened to any other employer in Canada," Brenda Seraphim figures. "Most people join a union because of how they're treated and in that case they joined because in that town to belong to the International Woodworkers of America was prestigious. They sponsor baseball teams and scholarships; they're very involved in that community." Within a couple of months of the store's opening in 1998, the employees had agreed to sign up with the IWA.

Brenda Beecroft was devastated. She determined to react sensitively, "doing a lot of watching and listening, being supportive to the team members, even the ones trying to do the most damage to the company. People are smart and saw how I was treating them." The union – which had promised them more than double the wages the company offered – soon stopped bargaining because the employees weren't supporting it. "The law was ten months before decertification could happen, and it had to be in that tenth month the team members applied to decertify. We had a hundred-per-cent decertification. The woman from the Labor Board said she'd never seen that before." As she tells the story, Brenda Beecroft's eyes glisten with tears.

ADVANCE AUSTRALIA FAIR

From the beginning, a hundred-per-cent union presence was a fact of life in all the company's stores in Melbourne. But there were other reasons why they were performing below expectations for several years. Replacing Craig Rasmussen there was Chris McGonigal, who'd started with Savers as a part-time cashier in B.C. in 1989 and was a Calgary store manager when the call came in 2002 to become Australian operations manager. Hard as she worked over six years to change the pricing structure and enhance the store environments, growth was at a standstill. Both Tom and

Donna McMaster, Australian managing director

Ken realized that perhaps importing managers from Canada wasn't the way to win the country.

"Australia is very exciting for us," Ken says. "I convinced the board to make a commitment to Australia and after a long search we hired a managing director, a native of the Melbourne area – and we've never had a local in charge of the business. Now we have this very talented woman, Donna McMaster."

She came with fine credentials. Growing up in a rural area an hour east of Melbourne, she was finishing high school and looking for work when someone gave her an application form for a management-trainee position at Myer Grace, Australia's largest department-store chain. Launched in 1900, the company is an institution there, like Macy's or Nordstrom in the U.S. Donna worked her way through various management roles, from sales to customer service, before becoming a store manager at a tender twenty-five – in northern Tasmania. The island off southeast Australia has fewer than 600,000 residents. Her store had about 300 employees and did about $70 million in annual sales. She did so well off that beaten track that she was soon general manager of the Brisbane store, with 1,500 staff and $200 million in sales, and then the men's-wear buyer in Melbourne with a $300 million budget serving seventy locations. In all she spent fourteen years with Myer Grace, with eight weeks' timeout to take a prestigious executive MBA program at the University of Virginia with students from eleven different countries.

She came back from that to become general manager of marketing and human resources and then VP of marketing. A bit burned out, she left to live with a family in Italy and learn Italian. On her return she became GM of retail development for a property-management firm in Melbourne – which is where she was when a headhunter called her about this unknown North American company called Savers.

"I saw it almost as the new frontier in retailing," she remembers, "with a philanthropic soul to the company in terms of its work with non-

The Frankston store in Melbourne won an international award for best store standards.

profit partners and its recycling and forwarding merchandise to underdeveloped nations. Wouldn't it be nice to have an executive position where you knew, at the end of the day, you are making a difference in the lives of people less fortunate than you?"

Checking out the five stores, Donna saw they ranged from "a couple of locations that had tough environments, like concrete floors and a cavernous warehouse feeling" to the Frankston store that recently won an international award for best store standards – "many people would shop in there without realizing it was a second-hand retailer." She was hooked and flew across the Pacific for six weeks' immersion in the Savers world in the U.S. and Canada. Among other lessons, she learned some of the corporate story from veteran manager – "and real character" – Tony DiMaina "I think it's very important and rewarding to understand the history and catch up on what you've missed out on," she says.

Her early plans were to increase the marketing reach – "We do about a million customer transactions a year in five stores nobody knows much about" – and finding other partners besides Diabetes Australia, which delivers about 120,000 OKs a year (generating as much as thirty per cent of the non-profit's revenue). "And I agree with Ken in that if peo-

An Australian newspaper said Savers is "mandatory for your next wardrobe update."

ple knew about us, what a difference it would make. We've just taken the model from North America and purely applied it here and there's much about Australia that is different. Eric Farley [who met with her in Australia] and I were talking about the level of presentation and the store environments of many of the discount operators being at a much higher standard even than North America. If we're going to be market-driven, then we need to lift our game, perhaps proportionately more so than the rest of the company in order to be competitive here. And again focus on our non-profits and some of the limitations that they face: labor and infrastructure and construction and property costs here are far greater than elsewhere. That does not mean that we cannot be successful, but we have just got to think a little bit more laterally about how we make the model succeed here."

Soon after she came to the company, she was seeing real parallels between her former employer, Myer Grace, and Savers. "When I first joined the Myer organization, members of the family were still participating in the company and on the board. It was becoming a very big company, but the values and the presence of the family that founded it had created a really terrific culture. I feel as I am getting that opportunity again. I've not had the honor of meeting Bill, but the presence of Tom and the core values that grew the business seem still very much part of the way in which we're going about what we do. With that said, I equally feel that we are on the cusp of moving from a family-run small business to a very large global enterprise and exploring some of the things of a particular interest to me. I love building things."

Encouraged by Donna's presence, Ken Alterman says, "Australia is a green-field opportunity to add two to five stores a year. Maybe a couple in 2006 and five in 2007. We've got to build up the organization to do that and find a few more [charity] partners. That's going to be Donna's big challenge."

Tom Ellison is just as bullish about the Land Down Under: "We will never be as profitable there store by store as we are here, but it is still a great opportunity – and it's a fifty-store market at least."

COMES THE FUTURE

When Ken came on the scene in 2002, Rod VanLeeuwen had gladly stepped down as president while remaining a director and an executive advisor on planning, development, and real estate. Tom would miss his close partnership with Rod: "He and I are very different people and come to a decision very differently – and that's good. I like people who will challenge me." Tom soon began to sense some of the same kind of relationship with Ken and felt more confident about having his own office a couple of blocks away from Savers' headquarters in Bellevue.

There he runs Legacy Commercial, a smallish entrepreneurial real-estate venture. It provides full-service brokerage and asset management for a closely held portfolio of commercial properties. Legacy evaluates new opportunities, brokers acquisitions and dispositions, and manages the corporate assets, property, and leasing. Tom took with him Savers' former CFO, Bill Fraser, property deal-maker Walter Scott, and the all-around Mike Griffith (who has since left to become a corporate manager and financial advisor for John Bacon). And working with him as an assistant property manager is his twenty-one-year-old daughter Jeni Ellison

("She can carry herself a lot better than I could at her age"). Her sister, Casey, three years older, is in medical school.

Of course, Tom continues to keep a relentlessly watchful eye on the company he co-owns with Berkshire Partners and the tack of Savers' journey under the steerage of its new president and CEO, Ken Alterman.

In 2003 the company bought nine locations of a thrift-store chain in western Washington called Shop & Save, which brought the number of Savers outlets briefly to 200 (although four were later closed while four became Villages and one kept its original name). "Over the next four years," Ken says, in a stream of consciousness, "I can see us opening up maybe forty stores, predominantly in the States, although we're finding more densities in Canada that work. In the U.S. the Northwest is probably our strongest area. Then Phoenix and the Southwest in general, then the Midwest – Minnesota and branching into Wisconsin, where we have fabulous quality supply and partnerships. And we should have six more stores there. New England with its giant population base. The South will be three to five years out as an expansion market. We need to go in big. We've got two stores in L.A., and they both struggle because it's been difficult to source the talented people and we've had difficulty with partnerships there. The same thing with Missouri. But Denver's doing well.

"The growth potential for us in the States is really to be four or five times larger than we are. We're working on some different models – smaller stores with central processing so not every one would have its own production centre. We would produce in a warehouse, which would also be a consolidation center where the rags come in to ship for export. If you can find the right twist to make this work, you can add 100 to 150 stores fast because all you're doing is creating a sales floor. I'm really hot on that idea; over the next couple of years, it's a work in progress."

In mid-2005, the store count was officially back up to 200 as a new Village opened in Richmond, B.C. Tom, the visionary who long ago projected that many company outlets, has his own dreams: "This could be a thousand-store chain. It should be, it deserves to be, and financially the company is very strong right now. That's partly the reason that I took on Berkshire – it has a lot of what they call "dry powder" [cash reserves to cover future obligations] to help us grow."

And after Australia, where else in the world will Savers spread?

"The reason we're working things out in Australia is because we don't deserve to go to a fourth country until we succeed in the third. We have obviously succeeded in the second one – Canada – but I can also see a lot of opportunity in the United Kingdom. The U.K. would be a knockout – Costco does particularly well there, for example." (He's friends of the principals of the warehouse-club chain based in nearby Issaquah, Washington, and knows it generated $2.6 billion in sales outside North America in 2004 – eighty per cent of that from its fifteen U.K. outlets.)

And then maybe even Europe?

"Not maybe – for sure. I already know where we'd start: the Netherlands. It has a tremendously high English-speaking content and the Dutch are used to the big-box retail concept. The rest of Europe would be spotty after that, but we could put other stores on the continent. The predominant growth of Savers, though, will occur in the U.S. There is no question in my mind that this company, going forward, can totally succeed."

As it has ever since his father's first Purple Heart Thrift Store in the Mission District of San Francisco (total revenue on opening day: $448).

...AND A FAREWELL

And what of William Oliver Ellison – WOE to many of his friends – who created this company fifty years before?

He and Carole now divide their retirement years between a beloved home on Lake Washington and winter getaways in Phoenix and Maui. Bill plays a little golf and gets good walking in with their dog, a tiny Shih Tzu named Chi Chi. For more than fifteen years, the couple have celebrated the day after Christmas and other occasions throughout the year with the extended family of Bob and Linda Cornyn, who have adopted dozens of children, many with special needs. Bill met them at an awards ceremony where Linda was accepting an honor while her husband, a master sergeant who'd served in the Korean War, sat in the audience helping one of

At the fiftieth-anniversary celebrations in 2004, founder Bill Ellison applauds the people who helped him make Savers Inc. the astonishing success it is.

their kids breathe with a mechanical aspirator. "It just melted Bill's heart," Carole remembers. He asked how they could help and the Cornyns told them to simply come visit. Ever since, the Ellisons buy gifts for the children – thirty-five of them the most recent Christmas – and hire a Santa to hand them out at the Cornyns' home in Puyallup, Washington. One year Bill and Carole arranged to have the couple stay at their place in Maui for a break from family, only to learn that the devoted parents had taken a couple of their kids along.

Despite his absence from the office, Bill isn't forgotten as the company's founder. As Savers prepared for its golden anniversary in 2004, he sat down in front of a video camera and reminisced about his family and the birth and the flourishing life of their remarkable business. Speaking of his son Jeff's early departure from the company, he said, "I had to realize that's life and children move on. They become real people." About Tom: "Within the first five years, I had a choice of getting run over or getting out of the way." And of his own leavetaking: "Retiring – that was a hard time. But there could only be one head guy in a company."

Bill received a small part of his due at a managers' retreat in Cancun marking the half-century of personal and corporate success. He was the surprise guest, and after his videotaped reflections about the astonishing story of Savers and Value Village, he gave a brief talk in person. "At one point," Ellen says, "Tom pulled a little camera out of his pocket and took pictures of his dad. It was them sharing the pride of fifty years in the company. I don't suppose there was a dry eye in the house."

The people at the retreat and so many others who'd worked with Bill Ellison over the years knew that his living legacy is an evergreen company that combines private enterprise with a social conscience. A company of more than 8,500 men and women concerned about providing families with fair prices for good clothing, a cornucopia of miscellaneous merchandise, and sometimes treasures. Rescuing the castoffs of an affluent society, reducing the depths of our landfills, and recycling our excesses to benefit the needy of other nations. And, perhaps most important of all, partnering with non-profit charities in our communities who offer the poor, the ailing, and the disadvantaged the gifts of human comfort, practical assistance, and financial support.

'P.S. I ♥ You'
POSTCRIPT

Each new generation seems to discover the stores of Savers Inc. for itself. Half a century after Bill Ellison opened his first outlet in San Francisco, a quarter-century after he opened his first Canadian Value Village in Vancouver, the following article appeared on the Internet – a means of instant communication barely imagined in the mid-1950s. The author, Haley Mlotek, is a University of Toronto student and a fashion commentator for andPop.com, an entertainment and technology news website.

There are some people who prefer to do their shopping in tastefully decorated boutiques, where the staff is paid to fawn over you and a pair of socks is $22. I am one of those people.

Then there are people who prefer the bare white walls, fluorescent lighting, soothing voice of Bryan Adams, and zombie death employee stares of – shudder – discount shopping. I have never been one of those people. Winners terrifies me and Wal-Mart, though it has a certain charm despite the mass-produced conglomerate evil etc., is both morally and fashionably wrong on all levels.

However, there's an exception to every rule, and my exception to the "no fluorescent lighting" rule is Value Village. For some bizarre unexplainable reason, Value Village provides me with a kind of calm and peace of mind that I previously only found in Ashtanga yoga. The huge second-hand store can offer me the same tranquility but no locked kneecap if I do the Downward Dog incorrectly.

It's a mystery to me how I can ignore the sound of Bryan Adams and other lite rock crap pumping through the intercom and the bare store walls, but maybe it's because you can find genuinely good merchandise there. Granted, you're going to have to dig through the fringed ponchos, old Danielle Steel novels, and mugs with pictures of the Pope on it, but underneath all that is a world of treasure. Particularly the children's section – some of my favorite tee shirts were previously owned by Pokemon masters and Harry Potter fanatics. Half the time I can't tell the difference between the tees I get for anywhere between forty-nine cents to $2.99 and the faux-vintage they're always pushing for $30 at places like American Eagle. I'm not trying to be all preachy 'cause I'm not buying something mass-produced or spending $30 on it, it's just logic. If I only spend a dollar on a tee shirt, then I have more money for better mass-produced clothing (i.e. another pair of gaucho pants, even though those are sooo last week).

The other great thing about shopping at your local Value Village is that you're probably going to find something that you have some emotional connection to . . . . For example, I found a gym shirt from my elementary school and a tee from my favorite childhood arts camp. I think it's always better to wear something that you actually have feelings about, as opposed to something sparkly with a fake ad for a fake ice-cream store.

In total, I purchased one sweater, one cardigan, one super-comfy bathrobe (so comfy it makes me sleepy), five tee shirts, seven almost-new books I've been wanting to read, and an old but still functional Operation board game. Total cost? Forty dollars and seventy-one cents. If that's not a good deal, nothing is.